# The Garden That Cares for Itself

Created and designed by
the editorial staff of
ORTHO BOOKS

Project Editor
**Norm Rae**

Writer
**Greg Williams**

Designer
**Gary Hespenheide**

# Ortho Books

**Publisher**
Edward A. Evans

**Editorial Director**
Christine Jordan

**Production Director**
Ernie S. Tasaki

**Managing Editors**
Michael D. Smith
Sally W. Smith

**System Manager**
Linda M. Bouchard

**National Sales Manager**
J. D. Gillis

**National Accounts Manager—
Book Trade**
Paul D. Wiedemann

**Marketing Specialist**
Dennis M. Castle

**Distribution Specialist**
Barbara F. Steadham

**Operations Assistant**
Georgiann Wright

**Administrative Assistant**
Francine Lorentz-Olson

**Technical Consultant**
J. A. Crozier, Jr., Ph.D.

Address all inquiries to
Ortho Books
Chevron Chemical Company
Consumer Products Division
Box 5047
San Ramon, CA 94583

**Chevron Chemical Company**
6001 Bollinger Canyon Road, San Ramon, CA 94583

# Acknowledgments

**Consultant**
Tom Eltzroth

**Illustrator**
Cyndie Clark-Huegel

**Photo Editor**
Sarah Bendersky

**Copy Chief**
Melinda E. Levine

**Editorial Coordinator**
Cass Dempsey

**Copyeditor**
Hazel White

**Proofreader**
Toni Murray

**Indexer**
Trisha Feuerstein

**Editorial Assistants**
Deborah Bruner
Nancy McCune
John Parr

**Layout & production by**
Studio 165

**Composition by**
Laurie A. Steele

**Separations by**
Color Tech Corporation

**Lithographed in the USA by**
Webcrafters, Inc.

**Special Thanks to**
Dr. and Mrs. John McChesney
David and Lisa Kruse
Janet Edwards
Tony Wessling
Orchard Supply and Hardware
Mudd's Restaurant and gardens
Elinor Moscow

**Photographers**
Names of photographers are followed by the page numbers on which their work appears. R=right, C=center, L=left, T=top, B=bottom.

William C. Aplin: 84L
M. Baker: 13BL
Liz Ball: 16, 24R, 44
Laurie A. Black: 27T, 27B, 57
John Blaustein: 12, 13BR
A. Boger: 32L
Kristie L. Callan: 84R
R. Christman: 67
Josephine Coatsworth: 1, 22, 30, 62
M. Cummings: 32R
Derek Fell: 65, 76L
Barbara J. Ferguson: 19R
Nelson Groffman: 31TL
Saxon Holt: Cover, 7R, 10L, 10R, 11, 19L, 20, 21, 25, 26, 28, 29, 34L, 35, 36L, 36R, 37L, 37R, 42, 43L, 46, 55B, 56B, 59, 60, 64, 66, 76R, 79, 80, 88, 90T, 90B, 91TL, 92, 93, 98, 99, 101, 102R, 103L, 103TR, 106B, Back Cover TR, Back Cover BL
Tony Howarth: 89
Michael Landis: 40, 47, 54, 55T, 58, 74, 75BR, 77L, 91R, 94, 103BR
A. Millard: 24L
Michael McKinley: 7L, 8, 15TL, 15TR, 33, 34R, 38, 70, 72L, 72R, 73R, 77TR, Back Cover TL
Ortho Information Services: Title page, 4, 6, 13T, 15BR, 31TR, 31BR, 43R, 45, 51, 52, 56T, 69T, 69B, 75BL, 77BR, 82, 84L, 85L, 85TR, 85BR, 86R, 87TL, 87TR, 87C, 87B, 91BL, 95, 96, 102L, 104, 105, 106T, 107L, 107R, Back Cover BR
A. Subarese: 81L
L. Swezey: 53
Valan Photos: Arthur B. Burchell, 14; Dr. A. Forguhar, 68; V. Whelan, 86L

**Front Cover**
Once established, the low-care pearl bush, azaleas, herbaceous plants, and evergreens create a lovely garden setting.

**Back Cover**
**Top left:** Woody ornamentals are easy to care for and blend harmoniously with other elements of the landscape.

**Top right:** Informal flower gardens are easier to care for and can be just as eye pleasing as more complex, formal ones.

**Bottom left:** Smaller and more sophisticated power tools make landscape maintenance easier for the home gardener.

**Bottom right:** Ground covers do not need the constant maintenance that a lawn requires.

**Title Page**
Colorful ground covers can provide low-care borders for garden paths.

# The Garden That Cares for Itself

# An Introduction to Low-Care Gardening

*Would you like a beautiful home landscape and a productive food garden that practically maintain themselves? If you've been spending long hours mowing, watering, weeding, pruning, and generally coddling the plants in your yard, perhaps it's time to transform your present high-care landscape into a more attractive low-care landscape.*

Seemingly endless routine chores can keep you from more enjoyable and creative gardening tasks. By minimizing the time required for humdrum maintenance, you can maximize the time available to enjoy gardening. This book will help you to create and manage a landscape that both looks better and is more productive when given less care.

Low-care gardening doesn't mean neglecting the garden or cutting corners. In fact, it often demands more thought and planning (and usually a larger investment in site preparation, plants, tools, and equipment) than high-care gardening. The aim is not to scrimp on maintenance, but, instead, to choose low-care plants at the outset, to place them in such a way that they are as self-maintaining as possible, and then to use laborsaving tools to reduce maintenance time even further.

*A striking landscape is created where small lawn areas accent low-care ground covers, shrubs, and trees.*

*Fruit trees have no place in a low-care landscape; keeping the surrounding area free of dropped and often rotting fruit requires too much attention.*

## CREATING A LOW-CARE GARDEN

When gardeners choose low-care garden features, they shun trees that drop messy fruits, for example, and they choose durable construction materials, such as stone and concrete, rather than temporary materials, such as untreated wood. These gardeners place trees in beds, where they won't have to remove the leaves, instead of in lawn areas. And, they use laborsaving equipment, such as automatic or semiautomatic irrigation systems, to cut the time they spend on routine chores.

Some landscaping features are inherently self-maintaining; others require constant maintenance. Use this book to guide you in choosing the former and avoiding the latter.

### Striking a Balance

The law of diminishing returns holds in gardening as well as in economics: The closer you approach perfection (exact bloom timing, flowers and foliage absolutely untouched by pests and diseases, or maximum vegetable yields), the harder it becomes, and the more time it will take, to get even closer. If you strive for a perfect garden, forget low maintenance! Self-maintaining landscapes work best and save you the most time if your attitude is midway between neglect and fastidiousness.

The ultimate, but not very inviting, low-maintenance landscape would not contain plants, just concrete pavement. Yet, woodland areas don't need much more attention than paved areas. Massed shrubs also require very little maintenance time. Maintenance time can also be kept low by restricting the area devoted to beds and borders.

A low-care landscape needn't be entirely filled with plants and other garden features selected primarily for ease of maintenance. It's fine to have some high-maintenance areas, but they should occupy only a small part of the landscape. Traditional home landscape designs burden their caretakers with large high-maintenance areas and small low-maintenance areas. If you don't want to be a slave to your landscape, you need to break with tradition.

### The Trade-offs

Creating a self-maintaining landscape involves a few steps: understanding and improving the site, determining which low-care plants and furnishings are appropriate for it, installing those components sensibly, and choosing suitable laborsaving techniques, tools, and equipment. Each of these steps requires research, foresight, and, inescapably, some time and money. However, by making these initial investments, you'll accrue timesaving dividends for years to come.

The alternative is to spend countless hours maintaining a landscape that is likely to be both less attractive and more costly in the long run, even though you pamper it. Today, most home landscapes are dominated by plants that are inexpensive and quick to establish—the very plants that usually require frequent maintenance. These landscapes are not for people whose time is valuable.

## ADVANCES IN LOW-CARE GARDENING

Recent developments in plant breeding, horticultural research, and agricultural technology have produced new low-maintenance gardening methods. These methods, coupled with the current preference for informal landscaping styles, make self-maintaining gardens easier to undertake now than ever before.

### New Varieties

Over the past few years, breeding and selection programs have produced an abundance of low-care plants. In this era of resource conservation, self-maintenance is a highly desirable characteristic of both ornamental and edible plants,

and it has become plant breeders' primary goal. Recently released cultivars require much less care than cultivars previously available.

### Efficient Techniques and Tools

Horticultural researchers have also recently developed some notable time- and cost-efficient plant care techniques, some of which contradict traditional recommendations. For example, transplanting a bare-root tree or shrub in the time-honored manner included adding some organic material, such as peat, to the hole, pruning back the top of the plant, and then staking the plant. Except in special cases, none of these procedures are called for by the newer techniques, a number of which are detailed and contrasted with traditional techniques in later chapters.

Technological miniaturization has come to home landscapes in the form of lightweight power tools and sophisticated irrigation equipment, some with surprisingly low price tags! Some of the more practical laborsaving tools and equipment are described in subsequent sections.

## CHOOSING THE MOST SUITABLE TECHNIQUES

No single low-care gardening formula suits everyone's situation. Your site, preferences, and constraints are unique. This book suggests many possible techniques for reducing landscape maintenance and will help you choose those that best fit your site and goals. Several of these techniques can be tried first on a small scale to see how they work. Some are inexpensive or even free, while others are quite expensive. Although the total investment of money and setup time required by a self-maintaining garden is typically higher than that required by a traditional garden, if you want or need to, you can make that investment over a period of time by expanding your low-care landscape gradually.

### Creating the Garden in Stages

Constructing a self-maintaining garden in stages makes such a project feasible even for extremely busy people, who, of course, stand to benefit the most from reduced maintenance needs. A good way to start small and easy is to transform a lawn area no larger than 100 square feet into a self-maintaining bed of trees and shrubs. This will give you a taste of what's involved in planning and installing different kinds of plants.

This book discusses the advantages and the disadvantages of different timesaving techniques to help you choose among them. Initial and ongoing costs, setup times, and skills necessary for implementing the various techniques vary widely. Assuming that a particular technique is suited to your situation, adopting it will save you some time even if you don't adopt any other techniques. Naturally you can expect to save additional time if you do adopt more techniques; only in rare cases are techniques mutually incompatible.

*Left: Planting massed shrubs rather than a large lawn or complex flower beds can help to limit maintenance chores. Right: Small, lightweight chain saws designed for home use make quick work of major pruning tasks.*

# Planning a Low-Care Garden

*Most of these general suggestions are gardening common sense, yet they are all too frequently ignored or carried out incompletely. Typically, they need minimal equipment, but they can require substantial time for research and thinking.*

S everal of these suggestions are appropriate in the initial stages of planning a new or renovated landscape. You shouldn't wait until it's too late to implement them. And don't think that the spring is the only time you can get started—planning is possible throughout the year. The fall is a good time for preparing beds, for removing undesirable plants, for installing some kinds of plants, and for having soil tests done. Spring is already crowded with outdoor work, so it's probably best to take your first steps toward a self-maintaining landscape in another season.

*A careful arrangement of living and nonliving ground covers creates attractive easy-to-maintain landscapes.*

*Left: A soil thermometer will help you locate the warm and cool areas in your garden soil and also the wet and dry spots. Right: A maximum-minimum thermometer placed in the garden will help you understand the seasonal variations of temperatures.*

## GETTING TO KNOW THE SITE

Don't begin planning a low-care landscape until you have taken the time to become well acquainted with your site. You need to understand its major climatic, ecological, and cultural opportunities and constraints. You probably won't know very much about your site within a few weeks, or even within a few months. If you must put in some plants quickly (perhaps your new house is sitting in the middle of a bare patch of ground), you'll have to rely on tips from neighbors and other local experts. Talk to extension personnel and nursery staff for advice on which easy-care species and cultivars are best suited to your area. You may eventually need to replace some of the recommended plants with better ones, but go ahead and do the best you can in the time available.

However, if you're converting an existing high-care landscape into a self-maintaining one, you have the luxury of taking as long as you need to become really familiar with the site's idiosyncrasies—another year of caring for the existing plants is a small price to pay to make sure that your design is sound.

### Collecting Data

Compile a record of frost dates, common weeds, plants most appreciated by neighbors, pest and disease outbreaks, and any unusual events such as damage from strong winds or from floods. Consider tracking temperatures in your garden. The time required to install and daily read a maximum-minimum thermometer will be amply repaid by a better understanding of seasonal variations. Use a soil thermometer to learn where the soil warms up soonest in spring, where it remains coolest in summer, and where to find the driest and wettest spots.

### Testing the Soil

Plot a map of the soil acidity around your site (inexpensive yet reliable handheld pH meters are available at most garden supply stores). Find out what soil type(s) you have. Have your soil tested for plant nutrients by your extension service or a private laboratory, but be aware that the results will probably vary widely for different areas of your site; you might want to have each relatively homogeneous area tested separately.

*PH is a measure of acidity and alkalinity on a scale of 0 to 14. The lower the number, the more acidic the soil; the higher the number, the more alkaline the soil. A handheld pH meter will help you determine the types of soil in your garden.*

## Learning About Plants in the Area

Make an effort to learn about the existing plants on your site and in the surrounding area, especially those that appear to be doing either very well or very poorly. Try to determine why some are having problems. Look for such causes as pests, diseases, insufficient winter hardiness, nutrient deficiencies or excesses, soil that's too acid or alkaline or saline, too much sun or shade, poor drainage, insufficient water, competition from neighboring plants, damage by wildlife or people. Pay particular attention to which factors vary throughout the year.

## Checking for Herbicide Contamination

Unless you've lived on your site for several years and know that no long-lasting herbicides have been used, you could have a problem if residual herbicides are in the soil. To check for herbicide contamination (which is commonplace when farm fields are developed), perform the following test. Sow ryegrass, tomato, and sugar beet seeds in a pot of your garden soil. If seedlings of all three grow and develop true leaves, you don't need to worry about residual herbicides that might damage landscape plants. Alternatively, ask your local extension personnel for help in determining whether the soil contains potentially damaging herbicides and how to neutralize them.

## Compiling Wish Lists

Getting to know your site includes becoming more aware of the wants and needs of the people and pets who will be using the space. After identifying the primary users, think about the site in terms of access, comfort, and function. An enjoyable way to move from these general considerations to decisions about specific landscape features is to ask the users (including yourself, of course) for cost-is-no-object wish lists. If you don't mention low maintenance, will the other users think about it as they compile their wish lists? Perhaps you should explicitly ask the other users how they rank low maintenance relative to their other desires for the landscape. The wish lists should give you a good idea of the wants and needs of all of the users.

The information you gather about a site's potential and the users' wishes will be invaluable for guiding your choice and placement of low-care plants, and for guiding your modifications of at least some existing site conditions. For a self-maintaining landscape, the right plant in the right place is first and foremost a plant that is well adapted to its immediate surroundings. If you don't gather enough information about the immediate surroundings, predicting whether a given plant will be well adapted is just guesswork. Of course, the plant will let you know, sooner or later, whether you guessed correctly! If your guess was wrong, the only remedy is spending more time on maintenance.

## CHOOSING THE LOWEST-CARE PLANTS

Choosing low-care plants that are exceptionally easy to grow is the key to establishing a self-maintaining garden. Here is what you should look for. Remember that the ideal low-care plant is well adapted to its immediate surroundings: climate, soil, other plants, buildings and other nonliving landscape features, and people. It also has an appropriate growth rate and mature size for its location; is easily established; has no special maintenance needs, such as training, staking, or frequent replanting; and is not invasive. The plant is naturally neat in appearance and doesn't drop messy fruit or leaves, doesn't interfere significantly with the growth of nearby plants, resists pests and diseases, and tolerates a variety of environmental stresses, including soil infertility, drought, and air pollutants. And the plant is readily available at low cost. A tall order indeed, but several plants listed later in this book come quite close to the ideal; they give high returns with little care.

### Seedlings and Quality Plants

It is easy to say that you should purchase only high-quality seedlings and plants—the ones that are unlikely to require time-consuming replacement. It is much harder to actually follow that advice. Judging the quality of mail-ordered plants in advance of their arrival is impossible. But you can improve the odds by refusing to accept dried-out, scraggly, or poorly rooted plants. Let it be known that first-rate plants are the only ones good enough for you. Reputable nurseries will get the message in a hurry, and provide you with higher-quality selections.

You can restrict your maintenance responsibility to only part of a plant's life cycle by purchasing seedlings instead of raising them yourself. Unfortunately, you can't always rely on commercial sources of vegetable and annual flower seedlings to stock the most desirable low-care cultivars. Hence, this book includes instructions for setting up a highly efficient seedling factory so that you can grow your own. Low-care bulbs, shrubs, and trees are relatively easy to purchase by mail order.

*Children's play areas, decks, and other features such as walkways and driveways should be taken into consideration when planning low-care landscapes.*

*Transplanting seedlings or small plants from a nursery or from one part of a garden to another are two timesaving alternatives to starting from seed.*

## Woody Plants

The best looking or biggest plant isn't necessarily the highest-quality plant. Contrary to the advice of some nursery people, it makes sense to buy small-sized woody plants because a smaller plant will have retained a higher proportion of its original root system when it was potted or lifted and will suffer less transplant shock. It's tempting to plant a large tree for instant shade, but as much as 98 percent of its root system might have been left in the nursery field when it was dug up. A larger plant might have a lush top, but it could have few roots and grow slowly for several years after transplanting. An initially smaller tree will resume normal growth much sooner and is likely to outgrow an initially larger tree within a few years.

## Transplants

One source of inexpensive low-care plants that is often overlooked is very close to home: your garden. You can move small plants from one part of your site to another with relative ease, and in the process, perhaps even transform them into lower-care plants. Here, *small* means less than about 5 feet high. Moving larger plants is possible, but you'll want to have professional help.

Before you start digging, confirm that the reason the plants are difficult to maintain is

*This colorful and somewhat formal garden takes advantage of grouping and zoning techniques that will make maintenance easier.*

their current location and that the new location will be significantly better. A good case can be made for relocating plants likely to grow too large for their current space, plants mistakenly planted in unsuitably wet or dry spots, and plants whose maintenance needs conflict with those of their neighbors. For best results, move plants when they are dormant. If you must move plants in full leaf, try not to disturb their roots (move soil balls with the plants), and provide plenty of water in the following weeks.

Perennials (other than grasses) generally need less care than annuals, but perennials can't match the showiness of annual flowers or the food productivity of vegetables, so you will probably want to include at least a few ornamental or edible annuals in a self-maintaining landscape. And annuals, whether edible or not, are wonderful for filling gaps between young perennials.

## GROUPING AND ZONING FOR SIMPLICITY

A fundamentally important rule for designing self-maintaining gardens is to avoid complicated plantings. This includes plantings with complicated spatial, blooming, or harvesting patterns. *Succession planting* (planting different species or varieties for a continuous bloom or harvest) and *intercropping* (planting one type of crop between plants of another crop) make for striking displays and efficient production, but at the expense of increased maintenance time.

Reducing plant intensity is a sure way to cut maintenance time. Limiting the number of different kinds of plants will also reduce maintenance time. You should avoid grouping together plants with significantly different maintenance schedules or pesticide and herbicide requirements and sensitivities, or you'll be returning to them time after time to carry out specialized chores.

It is much better to group plants that have similar maintenance needs, then you'll be able to mulch or to spray a particular herbicide in a single, quick pass. Grouping plants according to maintenance needs may sometimes conflict with aesthetic designs, but it doesn't happen often, since there are so many plants that are maintenance compatible and, grouped together, are also aesthetically pleasing.

## Group the Maintenance-Compatible Plants

Keep scattered landscape features, such as a shade tree standing on a lawn, to a minimum. Instead, group several maintenance compatible features together into distinct beds. Any grassed areas between the beds (the smaller these grassed areas, the better) will then be easier to mow, and there will be much less hand-trimming to do and less risk of plant damage caused by careless trimming.

**Minimize boundary lines**   Your goal should be to minimize the number, the extent, and the jaggedness of boundary lines that need to be maintained as sharply defined separators. Graduated boundary regions may require less time to maintain than sharp boundary lines; but whether your boundaries are regions or lines, try to keep them few in number, short in length, and as smooth as possible. Grouping plants is the easiest way to achieve low-care boundaries: for example, the boundary between a single bed containing several shrubs and the surrounding grass would probably be somewhat shorter and smoother than the

*A lone tree and a surrounding lawn (top left) require more care than trees (top right) standing in a well-defined ground cover area.*
*Bottom: Different shrubs with similar maintenance needs can be grouped to form an attractive low-care maintenance zone.*

many boundaries between individual shrubs and surrounding grass.

Taking a few moments to think about grouping and zoning will help you to strike a good balance between high-maintenance plants and low-maintenance plants, and also between plants and contructed landscape features. By making sure that you have zoned at least one or two small areas of grouped high-maintenance plants, you will avoid a dull look.

*Grouped together in a smooth-bordered mulched area, these evergreen trees require very low maintenance.*

And by zoning plant groups to complement constructed features, you will avoid a barren look. If you don't stop to consider these concepts, the temptation to pave over everything or to put a common fast-growing ground cover everywhere might win out, and you will be left with a self-maintaining landscape that is monotonous.

Zone realistically, but don't fail to zone in a bit of color and excitement!

**Design the boundaries for ease of maintenance** Boundaries in landscapes can't be avoided, but they can be specially designed for low maintenance. Although a graduated boundary, such as the edge of natural woodland, may require less maintenance than a sharp boundary, this isn't always true. Frequently, the lowest-maintenance landscape boundary designs are extremely sharp, and they are kept that way by constructed garden features.

Metal or plastic edging strips, which require little routine maintenance once installed, will keep grass from invading the sidewalk. Two side-by-side rows of bricks embedded flush with the soil surface will make it easy to mow grass that threatens to encroach upon a flower bed. A shallow, narrow ditch will stop many aggressive plants from spreading into a lawn.

## Establish Maintenance Zones

It is helpful to zone a site into areas deserving different levels of maintenance. You might want an immaculate area surrounding the front entrance to the house, but perhaps you could accept a reasonably neat area around the back entrance, and a not-too-disheveled area far to the rear of the site. Try to temper your aesthetic preferences with an appreciation of the functional requirements of particular areas. Front entryways are meant to impress; play areas in the backyard are not. One of the most common landscaping mistakes is mismatching maintenance levels and functional requirements—maintenance levels are almost always set too high.

Zoning shows you exactly how much space you are apportioning to intensively managed areas and how much to extensively managed areas. When you look at this information in the light of how those areas are being used, the mismatches can be startling. For example, are you treating your entire front yard as an intensively managed entryway? Have you placed an intensively managed flower bed adjacent to the childrens' sandbox? Can you bring the front boundary of the extensively managed area at the rear of your site even farther forward?

# Zone/Planting Map

A map of existing and potential maintenance zones around the home is extremely useful. It helps you determine which areas of the landscape will require different levels of care. A hand-drawn map need not be as elaborate as this example. A map can be redrawn several times; shift the components around until they suit individual landscape features and your maintenance goals.

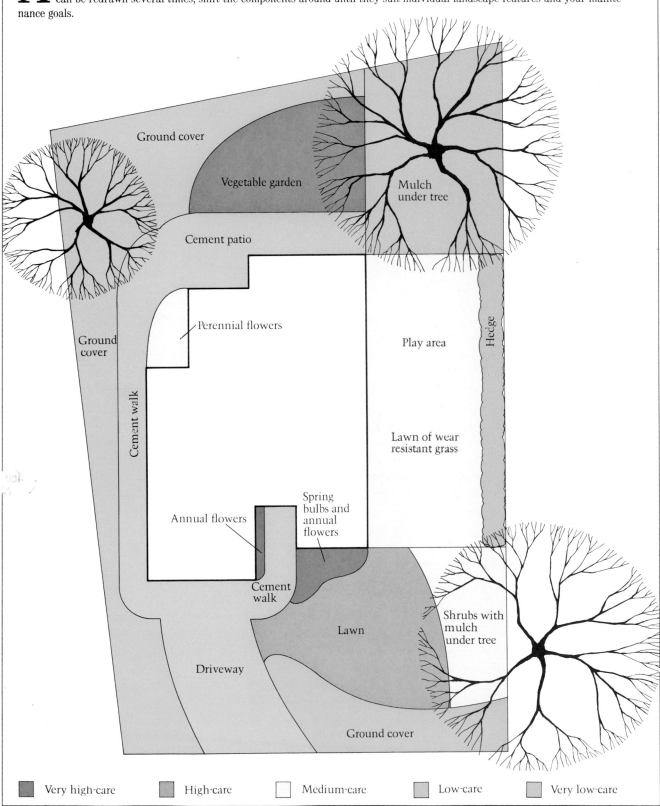

Ground cover

Vegetable garden

Mulch under tree

Cement patio

Perennial flowers

Ground cover

Hedge

Play area

Cement walk

Lawn of wear resistant grass

Spring bulbs and annual flowers

Annual flowers

Cement walk

Shrubs with mulch under tree

Lawn

Driveway

Ground cover

| | Very high-care | | High-care | | Medium-care | | Low-care | | Very low-care |

## THE RIGHT PLANTS FOR THE SITE, THE RIGHT SITE FOR THE PLANTS

You can tailor your choice of low-care plants to fit the site, or modify the site to suit the plants. The former is usually easier, but one or the other approach is essential to a successful self-maintaining landscape. Don't waste your time trying to grow bog plants on a dry knoll or acid-loving azaleas on alkaline prairie soil. You should create a landscape that fits your site, not a landscape pasted from somewhere else. In some cases, however, this rule can be safely bent a little.

Suppose your garden is already blessed with large trees that seem to be doing reasonably well, but aren't exactly low-care because of their heavy leaf or litter drop, pruning needs, or susceptibility to pests. Consider sparing them, for their shade will prove to be a useful tool for reducing maintenance. However, if you're determined to remove a large tree so that you have a sunny area in which to grow colorful annual flowers or a bountiful vegetable garden, choose the most-difficult-to-maintain large tree on the site, unless other considerations, such as soil quality, preclude this.

### Clues on Adaptability

You should have plenty of clues about the kinds of plants best suited to your site: which native species thrive there; which cultivated species appear to be doing best; which plants are favored by gardeners and professional growers in the area; which plants have a vigorous and healthy look in nearby parks and cemeteries; and which plants are recommended for their low maintenance by your local extension and nursery experts. By the time you've determined all this, you'll probably have a long list of well-adapted plants.

### Computer Programs That Help

Several computer programs are available that make plant selection and placement easier, though none are designed primarily for selecting low-care plants. Some of the programs will give you screen representations of your site so that you can see how your landscape will look when it is planted and how it will look in subsequent years. Computer databases are superb for organizing data on plant characteristics; they will help you to quickly identify the appropriate plants for a particular location. If you want to save time when designing your self-maintaining landscape, consider investing in one or more of the programs described on page 108.

## LOW-MAINTENANCE LAYOUTS

Landscape layouts can streamline or complicate maintenance activities. Ease of access to all areas of a landscape can shave minutes off the time it takes each week to care for your plants (remember, you'll sometimes be burdened with tools and equipment). In particular, many gardeners construct plant beds that are too wide (more than 4 or 5 feet) and paths that are too narrow (less than 20 inches for stand-up work, 32 inches for kneeling, or 42 inches for carts). There is also a more subtle reason for making wider paths: Since plants typically require more maintenance time than paths, in an easy-care landscape you should give more room to the latter than to the former.

A well-designed layout will also reduce maintenance time by directing pedestrian traffic appropriately. You should not deliberately channel everyone who comes to your door past delicate plants sensitive to the slightest hint of soil compaction or fungus spores imported from down the street—what horticulturists call "people-pressure diseases." It's much better to invite admiration of delicate specimens from afar—rather than next to the plant—especially if the admirers include children. People-pressures aren't limited to compaction and spreading diseases. Consider errant balls or Frisbees, misguided attempts to make sure the roots have enough water, and temptations to use up that last bit of spray on something, just so that it isn't wasted.

Mistakes in layout work the other way, too. In areas that must support high traffic, tough plants are advisable—but they shouldn't be too tough. Prickly, thorny, or aggressive plants in high-traffic areas will keep you constantly busy, protecting people from the plants!

## TOOLS AND EQUIPMENT

The correct tool is a joy to use and makes the job go more quickly. Given reasonable care, well-chosen quality gardening equipment should provide many years of service. In contrast, inappropriate bargain tools will slow you down

twice: while you're using them, and when you have to replace them (usually quite frequently and unexpectedly).

## Choose Tools and Equipment Carefully

The best choices aren't always the most expensive or the best looking, and there's no guarantee that they'll be found in the fanciest catalogs or stores. Almost without exception, the most serviceable gardening tools are those used daily by professionals. Ask some of the professionals at your local nursery where they buy their tools. If they don't stock professional tools, they will probably recommend mail-order companies that specialize in sales to nursery staff and landscapers.

Tools and equipment recommended for self-maintaining landscapes are discussed later in this book. These range in price from nothing to

hundreds of dollars, and their effectiveness in saving time also spans a tremendous range. It would be foolish to invest in every available low-maintenance gardening device, just as it would be foolish to invest in none of them. Those that appear to be most appropriate for your site and goals shouldn't be purchased casually (particularly if they are expensive); they might not work as well as they appear. Try to arrange a hands-on trial before you buy; at the very least, talk with people who already own similar tools or equipment.

## Provide Handy Storage

If you think this next suggestion sounds too simple to save much time, you're wrong. You can save many hours each year just by providing storage for gardening tools, supplies, and equipment close to where you use them most. Some gardeners place rural-style mailboxes on posts

*Left: Even the most self-maintaining or low-care landscape requires reliable tools. Select tools with an eye to their durability and ease of use.*
*Right: Properly chosen gardening tools will last a long time if cleaned after each use and stored in a convenient, dry place, such as this prefabricated toolshed.*

*Placed in convenient locations around the garden, rural mailboxes offer handy storage space for small tools, twist ties, labels, and other essentials.*

should be done. Make an effort to pare the calendar entries to a minimum number of truly important tasks—drop the make-work tasks that aren't necessary. Then, follow the calendar's suggestions.

Try to keep up with the gardening chores by scheduling frequent short-duration maintenance sessions. There's nothing like a catch-up session of a weekend-long duration to send even the most determined gardener back indoors for another month of neglect, which then creates the need for yet another catch-up session. In a pinch, don't hesitate to hire outside help to get back on schedule.

## Make a Map of the Site

Even if your memory is extraordinarily good, you'll save time by making a scale drawing of your site with the names of all the plants and the installation dates if you know them. Maps of vegetable and annual flower beds should be drawn separately each year, at a large scale. During the growing season, annotate these maps ("never came up," "flowered from July to frost," "disease prone," and so forth) for future reference. With this information at hand, you won't repeatedly plant species and cultivars poorly suited to your site, and you will quickly determine which are the low-care plants.

## Label the Plants

Most gardeners don't even consider labeling their plants, but labels, at least for perennials, are great time-savers. They'll save you countless trips to double-check the site map (which is better off left indoors, where it won't be damaged) before you start pruning or spraying for pests. Furthermore, sturdy metal labels, some on stakes, are available at low cost. It takes only a few minutes to install them, and they'll add a professional touch to your landscape.

Be very careful to remove the plastic name tags usually attached to woody plants purchased from nurseries. These tags can chafe bark and will eventually girdle limbs. It isn't a good idea to attach, even loosely, any kind of labels directly to plants.

around their property for storing small quantities of twist ties, labels and markers, string, and other essentials. Others place larger equipment storage cases or closets in convenient spots around the site.

## RECORDS, MAPS, AND LABELS

You'll save time if you keep written records of what works, what doesn't, and why. Use these records to make a calendar that will show approximately when particular maintenance tasks

## KEEPING TRACK OF LOW-CARE INNOVATIONS

Don't be afraid to try something new that might work better than your current methods. Horticulture is a progressive art and science, and laborsaving innovations are announced almost daily. Many of these innovations are great time-savers, as their developers and marketers claim; nevertheless, before you adopt them consider two questions: What are their costs? And what disadvantages, if any, are associated with them? The perfect labor-saving gardening technique (free and unproblematic) does not exist.

## New Releases by Mail Order

The newest advances in horticulture can take years, unfortunately, to reach local garden centers. Don't expect to find recently released low-care plants at a nearby nursery; you may have to order them from mail-order catalogs where the latest plants and equipment usually first appear on the market.

## Advice From the Experts

Try to make good use of whatever expert advice is available to you. Take that advice with several grains of salt, though, because most landscape architects, extension agents, and even some grounds keepers aren't familiar with low-care approaches to gardening.

By and large, designers are more familiar with high-impact plants than with low-care plants—after all, they don't have to maintain the landscapes they design. Extension agents generally spend their time helping to solve particular problems of high-maintenance home landscapes, seldom having an opportunity to consider low-maintenance alternatives. Grounds keepers for the most part aren't allowed to modify the high-maintenance landscapes they care for, so they become experts mainly at determining how little care can be tolerated by difficult-to-maintain plants.

The most useful advice you can get will probably come from seasoned plant experts who can inform you, sometimes in great detail, about the idiosyncrasies of particular species and cultivars: under what conditions they thrive, where not to place them, their good and bad habits, and so on. You will probably find these experts in the botany, horticulture, agriculture, and forestry departments of local colleges and universities. Chances are they'll be happy to try to help you—particularly if your queries are specific.

Some books, especially the larger gardening encyclopedias, are good for this kind of

information; however, the plant hardiness zones specified in many of them are at best suggestive, and at worst misleading. Your site might well be a zone or two different from what the maps show. Also, hardiness zone information won't tell you about bloom hardiness—whether a plant's flower buds are likely to survive temperature extremes at your site early in the growing season. Of course, flowers are the raison d'être for having most ornamentals; if they survive at your location but don't flower, replace them.

*Sturdy metal stakes with labels identify the plants and note when they were planted and other essential information that will make maintenance easier.*

# Low-Care Regular Maintenance

*Fertilizing, soil care, watering, pest and disease management, weed control, and tidying-up chores are absolutely necessary for attractive and productive home landscapes of all descriptions. However, these tasks are not ones many gardeners enjoy; most gardeners would rather be doing more creative, less repetitive, and more gratifying tasks, such as planning, planting, and harvesting.*

Although you cannot entirely avoid doing these unpleasant major maintenance tasks, you can cut the time you spend on them significantly. Just how you can do this is detailed in this chapter. Remember, you can pick and choose from these timesaving suggestions to suit your needs.

The more maintenance tasks you can do in the winter, the fewer you'll have to do during the busy growing season. Spreading the chores throughout the year won't reduce their number, but you will have more time when you need it most. Of course, some chores must be done during the growing season, but there are many that can be accomplished just as well, or even better, in the winter. For example, the best time to review last season's successes and failures and to plan for the new season is not in the spring—that's too late. Get a head start on your chores, especially soil testing. To avoid having to wait for the results, you should have your soil tested in the late fall or early winter.

*Every garden, including a low-care one, requires maintenance. However, the amount of time necessary can be reduced significantly without affecting the quality and productivity of the garden.*

*Left: In some cases replacing the topsoil, particularly in selected areas, is less time consuming than modifying the existing soil.*
*Right: Leaves falling into a bed serve as good natural fertilizer for the ground cover.*

## CARING FOR THE SOIL

It's unlikely that you would find it worthwhile to significantly alter or replace your subsoil, but poor topsoil (infertile, too sandy or clayey or rocky, wet, shallow, weed infested) should be modified or even replaced. In many cases replacing topsoil takes much less time than modifying it, and the cost of new topsoil may be less than you expect.

### Replacing Topsoil

Replacing topsoil generally entails simply adding a few inches of good soil on top of the poor soil. You may decide to add soil in selected areas only or to tackle the entire site if you're landscaping a recently developed site or completely renovating an established landscape.

You can even turn a solid rock outcropping or pavement into gardening space with a covering of topsoil. If you can be sure of proper drainage, annuals and smaller perennials will do very well there, provided that you're careful to maintain proper soil moisture and nutrient levels. If you have existing woody plants on the site, be careful not to add more than a couple of inches of soil or you'll risk suffocating the roots.

For partial renovations, and to avoid harming the roots of plants you want to keep, it's best to replace soil on a plant-by-plant basis. If you have a low spot where water collects, put a mound of topsoil on the spot and plant a tree or shrub in the mound, with the upper part of the root system above the natural soil. Or create a raised bed of topsoil. Pressure-treated wood edging, 3 to 8 inches high, will help to keep the topsoil in place.

**Purchasing topsoil** To keep maintenance low, the new topsoil must necessarily be free of weeds, pests, diseases, and toxic constituents. Don't buy topsoil of questionable pedigree—ask to see soil test results. At the very least, test the topsoil yourself with a pH meter, and take a sample to your extension personnel for visual examination. Find out exactly where the topsoil came from. Make sure you aren't replacing poor soil with soil that is just as bad, or worse.

Don't till the natural soil before you add topsoil, unless you need to improve drainage by breaking up a moisture-impermeable pan. Cultivation increases infestations of some perennial weeds by cutting each plant into many small parts, each of which becomes a new weed. Cultivation may also bring buried weed seeds to the surface, where they will sprout.

**Preparing the existing soil** Before you add topsoil, use herbicides to kill existing weeds and weed seeds in the natural soil. Annual weeds won't give you many problems after the topsoil is in place, since their seeds generally require light to germinate. But some perennial weeds have enough food reserves in their roots to enable them to grow up through the new topsoil.

Glyphosate herbicide kills perennial weeds effectively; it is applied when the plants are actively growing and translocates through the plants to destroy both aboveground and belowground parts. The safest time to use glyphosate around woody plants is probably in the fall. In trials with spring, summer, and fall applications of glyphosate around several ornamental

tree and shrub species, damage to those plants was least in the fall.

## Using Organic Mulch

If you place organic mulch directly on plant beds, you won't need to till the beds annually or to cultivate them frequently. The steady decay of organic matter into the soil will supply the minor nutrients your plants need and at the same time improve the soil structure. But you'll still need to add major nutrients (nitrogen, phosphorus, and potassium) and perhaps lime to raise the pH or sulfur to lower the pH, on a regular basis. If you add a lot of organic mulch (several inches each year), there will be less need for lime or sulfur; even acid-loving plants such as azaleas will thrive in soil with high levels of organic matter without periodic applications of sulfur.

## FERTILIZING

Some gardeners inefficiently move around enormous amounts of organic materials, such as manure or compost, to supply only a small quantity of nutrients where and when they are needed. The nutrients in synthetic fertilizers are more concentrated than those in natural fertilizers, so, for a given quantity of nutrients, synthetic fertilizers are less bulky and easier to handle. That doesn't mean that low-care gardeners shouldn't take advantage of natural fertilizers; it means that they should keep storage, moving, and handling of natural fertilizers to a minimum.

## Litter as Fertilizer

It's easy to figure out that catching your grass clippings and then spreading them again on the lawn is a waste of time. It's not so easy to see how time is wasted by raking leaves, shredding them, composting them, and then putting the compost back on the area from which you raked the leaves. If they decompose into the ground cover and don't exclude light, why not let the leaves stay where they fall? Leaves from some trees can indeed kill grass, but most trees in a self-maintaining landscape are dropping their leaves into ground cover or mulch. In this case, *litter* is just another name for fertilizer.

## Commercial Fertilizers

Your landscape will need more nutrients than the available litter-fertilizer can provide. To save time, buy ready-to-use commercial fertilizers instead of concocting your own by composting or mixing together various materials. However, be selective about which commercial fertilizers you buy—some make more sense for a self-maintaining garden than others.

**Slow-release fertilizers**  Slow-release fertilizers are ideal for self-maintaining landscapes, since they need to be applied only infrequently. They are available in natural and synthetic forms and, unlike highly soluble fertilizers, they won't cause burned (salt-damaged) foliage even if you accidentally apply too much. Application is quick—you simply broadcast the granular forms or bury the pellets.

*Slow-release fertilizers, in either granular or pelleted form, need be applied only infrequently.*

*Drip irrigation systems are a time-saving convenience. Once installed they require little attention, and they save water by reducing evaporation losses.*

## IRRIGATING

Semiautomatic and automatic irrigation systems that you can set and virtually forget about for most of the growing season are readily available at low cost. If you choose a trickle, or drip, system instead of an overhead sprinkler system, you'll save water as well as time, since you will greatly reduce evaporation losses and overwatering.

Once installed, some irrigation systems are essentially permanent. Other systems can be modified quickly and easily. You'll probably find that the latter, semipermanent, types are more suitable for a self-maintaining landscape because you can alter them as your plants' needs change. Semipermanent irrigation systems also tend to be much less expensive to install and maintain than permanent systems.

Be sure to keep a record of your irrigation system for later reference—having the record will save you time when you need to make adjustments or repairs. Trying to keep an accurate picture of the system in your memory will be difficult.

### Efficient Watering

Here are a few suggestions for more efficient watering, regardless of what kind of irrigation equipment you use.

☐ Place impermeable borders, such as metal edging strips, around irrigated areas to reduce water runoff.

☐ Divide your landscape into watering zones. Establish high-water-use zones for grass and large trees and low-water-use zones for other plants. If you water the entire landscape uniformly, some of your plants will be either too wet or too dry most of the time.

☐ As you are setting up the zones, take into account seasonal changes in shade, wind, and plant growth. You'll probably need to rezone at least once or twice during the growing season to avoid over- or underwatering.

☐ Never use high-volume irrigation equipment in small areas—if the flow rate of the equipment exceeds the soil's maximum absorption rate, you'll waste water in runoff.

☐ Automatic controllers are excellent for providing water regularly, but you must reschedule them during abnormally wet or dry periods or your plants will suffer and, perhaps, even die. Even in normal seasons, you should consider adjusting watering rates every month or more frequently.

☐ Low-maintenance irrigation systems aren't no-maintenance irrigation systems. Weekly inspections for small problems, such as leaks at hose couplings and especially clogging of drip emitters, will keep the number and duration of failures to a minimum. It pays to clean or replace any filters even more frequently than the equipment manufacturer recommends.

☐ Irrigate infrequently and deeply to avoid producing shallow, always thirsty root systems.

### Drip Irrigation

If your site undulates or slopes, you need to choose drip irrigation equipment carefully. Some emitters, including porous hoses, have poor pressure compensation, which means that the emitters at the lowest spots of the system

*Whirling-head sprinklers (top) and oscillating-arm sprinklers (bottom) are more time consuming to attend to than drip systems and waste water unless closely monitored.*

will put out much more water than those at the highest spots. Thus, plants at the base of a slope will receive more water than plants at the top of a slope. There are ways to offset poor pressure compensation when you are laying out an irrigation system, but it is much easier to use emitters with good pressure compensation. Ask your local suppliers about the pressure compensation characteristics of the various emitters they sell.

The tendency of drip emitters to become clogged varies widely among different designs. Discrete emitters tend to clog more easily than distributed emitters, such as porous hose. How often emitters clog also depends on soil characteristics, water quality, and irrigation scheduling. You may need to experiment to determine which kind of emitter is the most reliable

on your site. It might be best to install a test system with several different kinds of emitters in a small area. Then monitor their performance for a complete growing season before deciding on which emitter to use throughout the entire site.

### Water-Absorbing Gels

Commercially available water-absorbing gels (starch co-polymers, polyacrylamides, and polyvinylalcohols) are widely promoted as moisture-holding soil amendments and root dips for transplants. But in many field trials the gels haven't reliably aided plant growth after transplanting, and there is some evidence that they interfere with root aeration and the uptake of iron. But, gels may increase the time between waterings.

*Surrounding a planting bed with copper sheeting will keep away slugs and snails.*

## MANAGING PESTS

Your first line of defense against pests is choosing the right plants. Species and cultivars resistant to the major pests found in your area warrant consideration, even though some of the plants' other qualities might not be so appealing. Unless your pest control techniques and timing are virtually perfect (which requires a great deal of effort), pest-resistant plants will probably look nicer and yield better than pest-susceptible plants.

If the plants are susceptible to pest problems, sooner or later you'll need to spray them. However, you should think about prevention long before you consider control.

### Identifying Pests

The biggest mistake you can make is to use an ineffective control method. That will waste both time and money. So it's imperative that you first identify the pest(s) correctly. You can buy a magnifying glass and books that show you how to "key out" pests and damage symptoms, but it takes less time to get an expert opinion. Contact your local nursery or extension personnel; they will also help you to decide on the best methods of control.

Guessing which spray to apply is not appropriate: You won't want to start again from scratch. Nor will you want to start over because you didn't follow the label instructions or manufacturer's advice. In particular, don't try to second-guess pesticide label specifications for application rates; too much or too little can produce poor results and the undesirable side effect of destroying beneficial insects.

### Excluding Pests

There is a very low-maintenance technique for preventing pest infestations—exclusion. Often you can keep pests from reaching your plants by erecting a barrier between the two. There are many kinds of inexpensive barrier materials available, including wire screening and fabrics. Perhaps the most widely used materials are the nonwoven synthetic fabrics sold especially for covering garden rows. These lightweight fabrics let light and water through, but keep insects out, and they can be floated over plants without special supports.

Copper sheeting is very effective against slugs and snails. If growing beds are surrounded with copper sheeting, slugs and snails won't enter the beds because copper mildly shocks them when they touch it. You should be able to buy copper sheeting locally. In some parts of the country, heavy mulching, which is so important for self-maintaining gardens, invites mollusk infestations. If you live in the Pacific Northwest, especially, controlling slugs and snails by using copper sheeting, or molluscicides, or both is a prerequisite for any low-maintenance landscaping.

### Encouraging Beneficial Insects

Purchasing and releasing beneficial insects to control pests takes time that is better spent on other gardening activities, unless you have a hobby interest in biological pest control. Deciding what species of beneficial insects is needed and when to release them is a difficult problem even for pest management specialists; you are likely to see little, if any, return from the time and money you spend. However, it is easy to encourage the natural predators already endemic to your site. They know when to mate and hatch at your location; your main task is to avoid killing them. That means no wholesale spraying with broad-spectrum pesticides, which will kill beneficial insects as well as pests.

Whenever and whatever you spray, cover the smallest area you can so that you kill as few beneficial insects as possible (this will save time and money, too). Bide your time when a few pests appear. If you eradicate pests as soon as they appear, your beneficial insects will either die or go elsewhere, since you've eliminated their food supply. Give beneficial insects a chance to control the infestation. "Control" means keeping the pest

*Sometimes the quickest way to head off an insect infestation is to handpick the pests from the plants when you first notice them and their numbers are still small.*

population at a level low enough to maintain negligible plant damage. Start spraying only when plant damage is unacceptable.

## Introducing Companion Plants

Companion plants that repel pests have a long history and many advocates, but they aren't well suited to self-maintaining gardens, if only because they introduce an element of complexity that will demand extra time. Research also suggests that many plants traditionally claimed to be pest-repelling companions do not effectively repel pests.

## Altering Planting Times

If you have the time and inclination to experiment, you might like to try altering the planting times of annual flowers and vegetables to avoid peak pest populations. Perhaps you are even fortunate enough to live near an observant gardener who already has it all figured out for your area.

## Handpicking

Handpicking insect pests off your plants may sound time consuming, but it can be the quickest way to control a limited pest infestation.

Handpicking or knocking the pests into a container of water takes very little time in comparison to using pesticides. A technique more or less halfway between handpicking and spraying pesticides is spraying infested foliage with water—this will stop many kinds of pests (especially mites on roses) if you are careful to focus a fine, high-speed spray mainly on the undersides of the leaves.

## Setting Insect Traps

Traps are available for a few pest insects, but they are designed mainly for monitoring population levels, rather than catching large numbers of insects. Placing the traps and then maintaining them requires more time than most home gardeners will want to devote, unless, of course, the trapping becomes a hobby. Japanese-beetle traps are widely used by gardeners, but research has shown that they may attract more beetles to the immediate area than they capture, thus increasing damage to nearby plants. If you have a large yard, you might consider placing a beetle trap far away from susceptible plants, such as roses. If you use beetle traps, follow the directions carefully to prevent putting other plants at risk.

*When spraying any pesticide follow the directions on the container very carefully for safety reasons—and also to make sure the pesticide is the correct one for the plant.*

## Applying Pesticides

Systemic pesticides are registered for use on some ornamentals. After being applied (usually as a soil drench, as a tablet placed in the soil, or as a stake inserted in the soil), these chemicals move throughout the plants. Some afford good protection for long periods of time, since they aren't washed off by rainfall, and they aren't broken down quickly by sun or high temperatures. A new generation of systemic insecticides for edible plants is now under development, and the first product, derived from the seeds of the tropical neem tree, should soon be available commercially. Systemic pesticides typically cost more than nonsystemic pesticides, but their convenience and long-term effectiveness make them valuable for gardeners who want to save time.

**Using pesticides carefully** Some pesticides can damage plants if they are applied inappropriately. The extent of the damage will vary according to the combination of pesticide and plant; some pesticide and plant combinations are much more prone to result in phytotoxicity, or poisoning, than others. Be sure to check the instructions on the label carefully before applying any pesticide.

Always follow a few simple rules: Don't spray stressed plants. Don't spray on extremely warm days; phytotoxicity is probable if the ambient temperature is above 90° F. On sunny days, leaf temperatures can be as much as 15 degrees above air temperature. Be wary of applying pesticides during a drought or when temperatures are abnormally low; in general, slowly growing plants are more susceptible to pesticide damage. Spray when weather conditions favor rapid drying, not when humidity is high; the probability of plant damage is highest when pesticides remain in solution on plant surfaces for long periods. Avoid spraying mixtures; mixtures of pesticides can cause plant damage even though the individual pesticides do not. Keep your sprayer equipment clean; residues from previous sprayings can damage a different plant.

## Controlling Nematodes

Until recently, control of plant-damaging nematodes was labor-intensive, requiring applications of toxic soil fumigants under soil covers. However, Vapam®, a soil sterilant that kills diseases, insects, and weed seeds as well as nematodes can be mixed with water and applied with a watering can. In 1988, a nematicide derived from crustacean shells became available. ClandoSan® needs no special handling; it can be applied directly to the soil surface or tilled in, and no soil covers are needed. Note, however, that it gives off ammonia, which can harm plants, so it must be used only in fallow areas. Wait at least a month after applying it before you plant.

If you're having problems with harmful nematodes in soil around permanent plantings, try fighting them with leaves; pine needles are particularly potent. Mix the leaves into the soil for best results. Soil solarization will also help to control harmful nematodes; that technique is described in the vegetable gardening section of this book.

*Small animals, such as this raccoon (top left), can sometimes do considerable damage to plants and trees. If individual plantings are subject to injury from animals or birds, protect the plantings by surrounding them with wire fencing (top right) or by covering them with netting (bottom right).*

## Accepting Pest Damage

There is an invisible shield against pest damage that is absolutely free, a huge time-saver, and available to all who are willing to use it: It goes by the name of lowered expectations. Can you accept a little more damage to foliage, blooms, and produce than you've previously accepted? If so, you'll spend less time—perhaps much less time—battling pests.

## MANAGING BIRDS AND ANIMALS

Whether your location is urban, suburban, or rural, you're likely to experience some plant damage caused by birds and animals. You can try to prevent such damage by using either repellents (chemical, visual, and auditory) or exclusion techniques (plant covers and fencing). Exclusion is the only sure way to prevent damage: Numerous research trials and the experiences of many commercial growers have confirmed that repellents are almost never completely effective. Some repellents are highly effective for a short time, but then start to function poorly even if applications are renewed.

One possible exception is the bird-repelling balloon, originally developed in Japan. Basketball-sized with large bull's-eyes painted on it, this balloon has been praised by farmers and homeowners pestered by flocking birds (blackbirds, crows, and grackles). But it doesn't repel other kinds of birds—you'll need netting to keep them out of your fruit plants.

## Installing Fences and Nets

Fencing an entire garden isn't easy, but it may be easier and cheaper than fencing or covering many of the plants individually. A garden fence is also more permanent, since you won't have to adjust it as plants grow or as you replace them. And it isn't in the way when you do maintenance work or admire your plants. Of course, if only a few of your plants are suffering wildlife damage, go ahead and protect just them—or replace them with plants less subject to damage.

In some cases, easy-to-apply, inexpensive plastic bird netting is all that's needed to exclude woodchucks, raccoons, skunks, and even deer. To keep deer out of beds that contain low plants, such as strawberries, drape the netting over the plants and weight it down at the

*Left: Unlike wildlife, the family dog can be trained to stay away from planted areas. Right: Deer can be quite destructive in the garden, and sometimes the only way to exclude them is to erect a fence around the planting area.*

edges; deer will be afraid of becoming trapped in the mesh.

Bird netting can be difficult to use. Don't just throw a big piece of netting over plants; most likely, it will cause deformed growth and tangle when you try to remove it. Instead, staple or tie the netting to supports that will go around and over the plants; this is very effective. If a support frame isn't practicable, roll up the netting, place one end in position, and then unroll the netting over the plants. To make this easier, staple the ends of the roll to sticks. This way, the roll is easy to weight down or otherwise secure, and easy to store, too.

### Controlling Cats, Dogs, and Rodents

Pets can cause just as much damage as wildlife to ornamental and edible plants. Cats prefer to dig in soft and fluffy materials—organic mulches are ideal, unfortunately. Commercially available repellents aren't effective for very long, if at all, and fencing won't stop cats either, unless you cage the problem areas. The easiest solution may be to lock cats indoors; but think twice before you do this, since cats are your best allies for keeping in check vole and mole populations. Other methods of controlling voles and moles are, at best, only partially effective. Trapping and poisoning must be repeated over and over again.

Dogs sometimes dig, too, and they also cause damage to plants that is less obvious: poor growth caused by excessive potassium from their urine. Potassium becomes a problem in urban areas, where there are relatively few trees and quite a few dogs. Hose down the trunks of trees and shrubs with water if they are frequently visited by dogs.

Mulch is key to self-maintaining landscapes, but, improperly used, it attracts plant-gnawing rodents. Keep organic mulching materials away from plant stems.

## CONTROLLING DISEASE

Disease-resistant species and cultivars should be the first choices for plants in low-care landscapes. Your next line of defense is general hygiene. To limit the spread of diseases, follow three rules, none of which require much effort: Always dispose of all diseased plants and plant parts in the trash. Till or rake the tops of dead plants into the soil at the end of each growing season. Rotate annuals from place to place so that pathogens don't build up in the soil.

In the past few years, it has been discovered that organic matter, especially when combined with calcium, will kill some soilborne diseases. If you till or rake dead annuals and tops of perennials into a layer of organic mulch, you'll minimize disease carryover from year to year. Composting the debris will also kill the pathogens, but composting is much more labor-intensive. Soil solarization is another technique for killing soilborne diseases; it is described on page 92.

### Reducing Humidity

A number of diseases favor extremely humid conditions, especially if water droplets have formed on foliage or blooms. Drip irrigation is the best way to keep foliage and flowers as dry as possible during watering. If you must use a sprinkler or a watering can for spot-watering, water early in the day so that the plants dry off before dusk. The humidity around plants is affected by how closely they are spaced. To minimize the incidence of disease, give plants ample space (of course, this will result in more weeds unless you use mulches or herbicides).

Another way to reduce disease is to coat plants with water-impermeable films. On recent trials, polymeric antitranspirants have very effectively controlled powdery mildews and certain other fungal diseases, even on susceptible plants such as roses. The antitranspirants, which are actually marketed as antidesiccants, should be sprayed as a 2- to 3-percent emulsion every few days so that new growth will be protected. These chemicals have very low toxicity, and they are biodegradable, so preparation and cleanup take very little time.

### Fluoride Sensitivity

Fluoride sensitivity isn't exactly a disease, but its symptoms are diseaselike: burned leaf tips or margins and dropping of foliage. In 1987 the allowable concentration of fluoride in drinking water in the United States was raised well into the range of sensitivity for plants in the following genera: *Cordyline, Dracaena, Chlorophytum, Zebrina, Calathea, Maranta, Pleomele, Stromanthe,* and *Rosa.* If your irrigation water contains fluoride, watch out for disease symptoms on those plants.

Some plants can apparently tolerate high fluoride concentrations in irrigation water. These include chrysanthemums, carnations, tomatoes, and cucumbers. There is no easy and inexpensive way to reduce the fluoride in irrigation water. If your water supply contains too much fluoride for some of your plants, the best solution is to replace the most sensitive plants.

### Identifying the Disease

As with pest control, you need to properly identify disease problems before you turn to control measures. Plant disease diagnosis is a specialty of extension personnel, so don't hesitate to seek their help; they will also be able to suggest appropriate control techniques.

## CONTROLLING WEEDS

Weeds are weeds only in the eyes of their beholders (alas, that often includes the neighbors). No plant, even if deemed noxious in some areas, is always and everywhere a weed. A plant's status as a weed often depends on how it is grown. This fact can be used to great advantage in self-maintaining landscapes, where it makes sense to encourage the growth of some plants usually considered weedy. After all, your most persistent local weeds are truly low-care plants: They thrive even with absolutely no maintenance! This might sound like heresy, but have you ever considered encouraging weeds to grow and, in the process, reforming them somewhat?

### Weeds as Native Plants

Weeds (you might want to call them native plants in the presence of neighbors) are most effective in small areas. Aim for a fairly uniform stand of one or two kinds of weeds; an unkempt patch of several species might look too weedy. It even makes sense to mulch your

*A few species of native plants (or even weeds) can be quite attractive in a self-maintaining landscape if you can stop them from encroaching on other planted areas.*

*Weeds can be controlled by using the right kind of mulch. Peat moss mixed with topsoil (top left) does not inhibit weeds, whereas a bark mulch (top right) controls weeds effectively.*

domesticated weeds, to keep the coarser sorts at bay. You can encourage volunteer seedlings, or you can buy native plant seeds. Of course, the species already on your site are the best candidates in terms of self-maintenance.

### Undesirable Weeds

If you decide not to encourage weeds, you have many choices. Mass plants so that there is little room between them for weeds to grow—where there is a desirable plant, there is no weed. Where there is a rock, there is no weed. Where there is adequate mulch, there is no weed. Where growing conditions are extremely poor (no water, no nutrients, no light, toxic chemicals in the air or the soil), there is no weed. Withhold whatever nourishment weeds need to grow, and if that's not enough, use herbicides. In short, by making sure that every location in your landscape has a desirable plant, a rock (or an equivalent), mulch, or extremely poor growing conditions, you will banish weeds.

When a weed does appear, there's no advantage to be gained by postponing its demise. Larger weeds are harder to kill, whether you are pulling them or using herbicides. Attend to the young weeds without delay, and you'll never have any mature ones dropping more seeds. Weed seeds can also be killed by solarizing the soil; this technique is discussed later in this book, on page 92.

## MULCHING

Field trials of various mulches have shown that there is no single outstanding mulching material in terms of weed control effectiveness. However, mulches do vary in other ways, and their appearance, longevity, and availability are important in terms of maintenance requirements. For minimal maintenance, shredded bark and chopped leaves are good choices. The former is generally available at garden supply stores, but the latter is not. You can, however, chop dry leaves very quickly with a small power shredder/grinder. Another type of minimal-maintenance mulch is bagasse, or crushed sugar cane, sold by farm supply stores for chicken litter.

### Plastic Sheeting

Black plastic sheeting is very easy to handle, inexpensive, and also durable if it's covered with a layer of organic mulch to prevent sunlight from breaking it down. The sheeting should have holes punched in it about an inch apart to allow adequate root aeration and water penetration. The holes are essential if you aren't using drip irrigation equipment under the sheeting. Prepunched black plastic sheeting is available commercially, as are several similar weed barrier materials that are permeable to air and water. Otherwise, you can punch the holes in the plastic sheeting yourself with a sharp nail or knife.

## Organic Mulch

If you put organic mulch directly on top of the soil, without an intervening barrier, you may need to add additional nitrogen fertilizer. The existing nitrogen becomes "tied up" by microbes as they break down the mulch. A nitrogen shortage is most likely to occur if the organic mulch is high in carbon and very low in nitrogen—characteristics of bagasse and sawdust.

**Weed-contaminated mulch**  Beware of mulch contaminated with weed seeds. It's better to avoid questionable mulch (especially unsterilized manure) than to attempt to kill the weed seeds in it. You can compost or pasteurize it, but there's no guarantee that the final product will be clean. Sphagnum peat makes a clean mulch, but once it dries out, it is difficult to wet again, so avoid peat if you rely on overhead watering or natural precipitation.

**Paper and cardboard mulch**  Mulch doesn't need to have a fancy name or to come from a store: Paper and cardboard make excellent mulch if you lay drip irrigation under it. Water applied from above would have to soak through several layers of paper. Newspaper is fine; despite rumors to the contrary, its ink (black or colored) is not loaded with lead—you can use all the newspaper you want. It's best to mix other kinds of paper, however. Some types, especially glossy magazine paper with colored ink, do contain high concentrations of lead and other potentially toxic metals.

You'll probably want to cover paper mulch with a more attractive material. Choose organic materials, such as shredded bark, in preference to gravel and other materials that never decay. The latter look attractive when first installed, but they won't stay that way for long. Plant litter is highly visible in gravel and difficult to remove except by hand. Gravel also has a way of ending up outside beds, where it is all too obviously out of place and laborious to move.

## TIDYING-UP CHORES

A self-maintaining garden should have very few plants that produce litter. Nevertheless, it would be an unusual garden that produced no litter at all. One of the desired results of a low-care garden is the reduction of cleanup chores. Leaf raking, pruning, and other cleanup tasks

can be minimized by considering some of the suggestions in this section.

## Reducing Leaf Raking and Disposal

You can reduce the time you spend raking leaves and disposing of them by grouping deciduous trees and shrubs in beds that are separate from lawn areas. These beds can be carpeted with ground covers or organic mulches that swallow up most fallen leaves. If some of the leaves aren't quite out of sight, you might try raking or sweeping the ground cover, or mulching lightly, or hosing the area with water. Allowing the leaves to dispose of themselves in this manner also improves the soil in the beds. In the vegetable garden, you can till litter directly into the soil.

*Leaf raking is an unavoidable task, even in a low-care garden. From a wide variety of rakes, choose the one that will make the job as easy as possible in your particular landscape.*

*Gasoline-powered portable leaf blowers (top right) and vacuums (top left) make yard cleanup quicker and easier.*

Many types of power equipment are available to make landscape cleanup quicker and easier, such as rakes, blowers, and vacuums. For home use, portable backpack blowers are the most appropriate. These have enough power to send the few leaves that end up in grassed areas back into beds, where they become mulch without further treatment.

## Pruning Faster

Arborists in California have developed a labor-saving pruning tool, the axe-handle saw. It produces cleaner cuts on small branches than a chain saw and is much easier to maneuver than a pole saw. The axe-handle saw is easy to make: Simply bolt a fine-toothed pole saw blade onto a 3-foot-long single-bit axe handle. Or you

can cut off a pole saw, but that costs more, and the round handle provides less control. Experienced axe-handle saw users report time savings of 20 to 50 percent compared with standard tools. Slow-growing plants need little pruning. By choosing compact or dwarf species and cultivars whenever possible, you'll cut maintenance time requirements. Also, shade-tolerant plants usually, but not always, grow more slowly.

## Other Cleanup Tips

To trim wide hedges faster and to trim plants in the middle of wide beds without stepping in the beds, place rigid plastic tubes (PVC plumbing pipe works well), up to 4 feet long, over the handles of your hedge trimmers.

High-activity areas of the landscape that tend to become and remain cluttered, such as vegetable gardens and laundry areas, are best hidden from view. However, don't make the mistake of hiding those areas with plants, especially trimmed hedges, which require a lot of care. Durable fencing is a good low-care alternative to plants for screening.

In winter, keeping ice off pathways by spreading salt on them takes time, and the salt can harm plants. A low-maintenance alternative is installing heating coils under the pathways.

Don't be too easy on hard-to-maintain plants. If you find that a major portion of your maintenance time is going to a few plants or a few areas, consider a radical solution: Replace the plants or move them from the difficult-to-maintain areas. Remember, concrete requires much less maintenance than plants. If you aren't ready to go that far, try mulch without any plants.

Narrow beds allow easy access to plants, but they can be too narrow, especially if they contain rapidly growing plants. Instead of repeatedly pruning back plants that outgrow their beds, make the beds wider.

Finally, you really don't need to clean up every day, or even every week. Unless there's a problem with disease, you're better off consolidating cleanup chores in a single block of time. That way, you won't have to go to the trouble to get out and put back the same tools and equipment time after time.

*Rigid plastic tubes placed on hedge-clipper handles (top right) and an axe-handle saw (top left) speed up pruning chores and provide easier access to spots that are difficult to reach.*

# Low-Care Lawns and Ground Covers

*You can enjoy an attractive landscape containing low-care grass or ground covers, or a mix of the two, and spend much less time maintaining it than you would a more traditional landscape containing a large lawn area.*

The typical homeowner spends more time on lawn maintenance than on all other landscape and garden chores put together. Most lawns are anything but self-maintaining, because grass is inherently a high-maintenance ground cover. Lawns require frequent mowing, watering, weeding, fertilizing, pest and disease control, and raking. Thus, one of the most effective ways to save time on landscape maintenance is to have as little grass as possible.

*The lowest-care living ground cover is a meadow of native plants. One this size is probably impractical for most suburban homes, but smaller areas of properly controlled native plants can also be very attractive.*

*A low-care landscape would never contain a lawn this size because, in spite of its beauty, it requires a great deal of maintenance.*

## SETTING GOALS

There are many easy-care ground covers that you can substitute for grass in most climates. Mulched beds of low-maintenance trees, shrubs, herbaceous perennials, and a few annuals can fill smaller areas in place of grass. Hardscapes such as paving, concrete walks, and patios can substitute for grass in areas subject to high traffic.

The appropriate mix of grass and other living or nonliving ground covers depends on your personal preferences and goals. Here are some considerations to keep in mind when you're deciding how much to restrict grassed areas in your low-care landscape.

### Lawn Areas

Large expanses of lawn traditionally have been associated with desirable American home landscapes; therefore, in most neighborhoods, a yard with small grassed areas will be unique— at least until easy-care landscaping catches on. Consider yourself a pioneer, and be prepared to explain the laborsaving advantages of your design to those who might think it peculiar.

As a living carpet for outdoor work and play, grass has few peers. Nearly all the alternative ground cover plants are damaged by even moderate foot traffic. Hardscapes obviously withstand heavy traffic but, swimming pools and ball courts notwithstanding, they are hardly inviting for leisure activities. Thus, unless you're certain that you have no need for open areas that have good resilience to traffic, you'd better keep some grass—maybe for a children's play area or for a picnic area.

Some grasses are much more trouble-free than others. The chart opposite shows some maintenance characteristics of the most readily available cool-season grasses (adapted to the North) and warm-season grasses (adapted to the South).

### Low-Maintenance Grasses

Ask at your local nursery for recommendations on low-maintenance varieties of grass best suited to your location. Very likely, these won't be the most common varieties, because many low-maintenance varieties aren't as visually attractive as high-maintenance varieties.

The major turfgrass companies have made reduced maintenance an objective in their breeding programs. Extraordinarily easy-care varieties are becoming available, including some that need almost no mowing, little water, and minimal fertilizer. If the nearest retailer is unaware of the latest low-maintenance varieties, try elsewhere—you might save yourself hundreds of hours of work over the next few years.

## Nongrass Ground Covers

Nongrass ground cover plants, mulched planting beds, and hardscapes all cost more than grass to install—that's why they're seldom used to cover large areas in residential landscapes. However, in the long run, alternatives to grass actually can be cheaper than grass because of the lower maintenance costs. If you find the high initial cost of nongrass ground covers prohibitive, remember that you can eliminate grassed areas slowly and spread the installation cost over a period of years.

Nongrass ground cover plants tend to look somewhat less tidy during the growing season than does grass, particularly if they are given little attention. However, many of the nongrass ground cover plants hide fallen leaves and twigs (no raking needed), and the

## Characteristics of Various Grasses

| Characteristics | Cool-Season Grasses | Warm-Season Grasses |
| --- | --- | --- |
| **Maintenance needs for good persistence and density** (lowest to greatest) | Tall fescue, fine fescues, Kentucky bluegrass, perennial ryegrass, creeping bentgrass, colonial bentgrass | Bahiagrass, carpetgrass, centipedegrass, zoysiagrass, St. Augustine grass, Bermudagrass |
| **Wear resistance** (greatest to least) | Tall fescue, perennial ryegrass, Kentucky bluegrass, fine fescues, creeping bentgrass, colonial bentgrass | Zoysiagrass, Bermudagrass, Bahiagrass, St. Augustine grass, carpetgrass, centipedegrass |
| **Shade tolerance** (greatest to least) | Fine fescues, colonial bentgrass, tall fescue, creeping bentgrass, Kentucky bluegrass, perennial ryegrass | St. Augustine grass, Bahiagrass, carpetgrass, centipedegrass, zoysiagrass, St. Augustine grass |
| **Tolerance of high temperatures** (greatest to least) | Tall fescue, creeping bentgrass, Kentucky bluegrass, colonial bentgrass, fine fescues, perennial ryegrass | Zoysiagrass, Bermudagrass, carpetgrass, centipedegrass, St. Augustine grass, Bahiagrass |
| **Tolerance of low temperatures** (greatest to least) | Creeping bentgrass, Kentucky bluegrass, colonial bentgrass, fine fescues, tall fescue, perennial ryegrass | Zoysiagrass, Bermudagrass, Bahiagrass, centipedegrass, carpetgrass, St. Augustine grass |
| **Drought tolerance** (greatest to least) | Fine fescues, tall fescue, kentucky bluegrass, perennial ryegrass, colonial bentgrass, creeping bentgrass | Bermudagrass, zoysiagrass, Bahiagrass, St. Augustine grass, centipedegrass, carpetgrass |
| **Tolerance of wet soils** (greatest to least) | Creeping bentgrass, tall fescue, colonial bentgrass, Kentucky bluegrass, perennial ryegrass, fine fescues | Bermudagrass, Bahiagrass, St. Augustine grass, carpetgrass, zoysiagrass, centipedegrass |
| **Suitability for acid soils** (greatest to least) | Tall fescue, fine fescues, colonial bentgrass, creeping bentgrass, perennial ryegrass, Kentucky bluegrass | Carpetgrass, centipedegrass, Bermudagrass, zoysiagrass, St. Augustine grass, Bahiagrass |
| **Suitability for saline soils** (greatest to least) | Creeping bentgrass, tall fescue, perennial ryegrass, fine fescues, Kentucky bluegrass, colonial bentgrass | Bermudagrass, zoysiagrass, St. Augustine grass, Bahiagrass, carpetgrass, centipedegrass |
| **Tendency to produce thatch** (least to greatest) | Tall fescue, perennial ryegrass, fine fescues, Kentucky bluegrass, colonial bentgrass, creeping bentgrass | Centipedegrass, Bahiagrass, carpetgrass, zoysiagrass, Bermudagrass, St. Augustine grass |
| **Susceptibility to diseases** (least to greatest) | Tall fescue, perennial ryegrass, Kentucky bluegrass, fine fescues, colonial bentgrass, creeping bentgrass | Centipedegrass, Bahiagrass, carpetgrass, zoysiagrass, Bermudagrass, St. Augustine grass |

evergreen ground covers are often much more attractive than grass in winter.

## PLANNING GROUND COVER AREAS

A map of your site that shows both current and desired activity zones and traffic flow patterns is essential for deciding where to place grass and other ground covers for low maintenance. The most resilient ground covers, hardscapes and grass, are the best choices for areas with heavy traffic, such as entranceways, play areas, driveways, and paths. Less resilient nongrass ground cover plants and mulched beds of trees, shrubs, and herbaceous perennials should be reserved for areas with little traffic: along fences, screens, banks, and the edges of your lot.

Ground cover plants over a foot tall are a good choice along the borders of well-defined paths. They will help to regulate traffic and minimize the need for edging. Some pedestrians, especially children, will stray from paths bounded by low ground covers or mulch. Each ground cover area—grass or nongrass, living or not—should convey an unambiguous message: either "welcome" or "keep off." Pavement and closely clipped grass say "welcome"; tall ground cover plants say "keep off." So, plant blocks of nongrass ground cover plants with a diversity of heights that will keep foot traffic in well-defined paths.

### Determine High- and Low-Activity Areas

Think of the least accessible and hardest-to-mow places on your property; those are ideal for nongrass ground covers. To determine how far you can extend them before you run into high-activity areas, look for regions of low activity between high-activity areas. These areas are also ideal for nongrass ground covers. You don't need to avoid grass in all of these regions. And if they are all already grassed, you can convert them slowly, one or two at a time. Beware of introducing a monotonous appearance—too much of one nongrass ground cover can be as boring as too much grass.

### Establish Grass and Ground Cover Borders

Lay out the borders of grass and ground cover areas on a scale map of your site. Try to avoid sharp corners on the borders of grassed areas; smoothly curving borders save mowing time. Rounded borders also fit in nicely with the informal style of self-maintaining landscapes.

In general, the border region between two areas will require more maintenance, such as pruning and edging, than will the interior of either region. In the border region, it can also be difficult to satisfy the different requirements of different plant species; one species might need much more water or fertilizer than another. Therefore, try to keep the ratio

of border length to planting area as small as possible. Avoid beds with intricate shapes and undulating borders.

If your site map shows rather large areas of high activity, don't assume that your only options are to pave most of those areas, hire help, or give up on having an easy-care landscape. There are several techniques to reduce the maintenance needs of grasses; these are discussed later in this chapter.

## INTEGRATING LIVING AND NONLIVING GROUND COVERS

Nonliving ground covers, including mulches, typically need less care than living ground covers. The ultimate minimal-maintenance landscape would consist entirely of nonorganic mulching materials placed over weed barriers and construction materials such as concrete, asphalt, large stones, and preservative-treated wood. Such a hardscape is neither economically nor aesthetically attractive, and it surely isn't a garden. For a balanced site design, you should attempt to integrate nonliving ground covers with living ground covers and other kinds of plants.

The most practical approach to creating an integrated, balanced design is to begin by siting hardscape features where they are functionally appropriate and where access for maintenance is difficult. For example, pave sitting areas, high-traffic pathways, and areas around swimming pools and ball courts and under clotheslines. Place riprap on banks that are too steep to be maintained easily, and nonorganic mulch along street borders.

### Easy-Care Boundaries

Design the boundaries between hardscape features and planted areas for easy care. Pavement edges flush with the ground can be trimmed quickly with a lawnmower, but raised edges might require hand-trimming. Woody plants that produce considerable amounts of litter shouldn't be placed near pathways, driveways, or areas with light-colored nonorganic mulch. Plants that tend to lean over shouldn't be used to line pathways. Some of the nongrass perennial ground cover plants swallow large amounts of plant litter; under messy trees and shrubs, these are more suitable than nonorganic mulch. If you decide to devote much of your site to paved areas, consider buying a leaf vacuuming machine or a backpack leaf blower to speed up debris collection and disposal.

There are hundreds of plants other than grass that are ground covers: annuals, biennials, herbaceous perennials, shrubs, and vines. Some grow less than an inch high, others reach several feet. The best maintain a dense canopy over the soil during the growing season, completely shading out weeds. The maintenance needs of nongrass ground cover

*Borders between grass and hardscape features (top left) or between grass and ground covers (top right) should be designed for easy maintenance.*

*In high-use areas, such as an outdoor seating area, integrating living and nonliving ground covers can reduce maintenance needs while still providing attractive surroundings.*

plants vary greatly, ranging from extremely high for most annuals to extremely low for some shrubs and vines.

## Meadow Areas

In general, you should avoid annual ground covers, since they require replanting every year. However, there is an exception to this rule: meadow areas. Largely filled with native annuals, and possibly some nonnative annuals that are self-seeding at your location, meadow areas are exceptionally easy to establish. You need simply to till the soil (shallowly is fine), mulch lightly with straw or other organic materials to prevent soil erosion, and then either sow a commercial wildflower seed mix formulated for your location or rely on native plant seeds already in the soil. With only minimal attention, meadow areas can become elegant alternatives to grass.

What are the differences between a meadow area and a common weed patch? First, meadow areas should have well-defined permanent or semipermanent boundaries, such as brick edging set flush with the soil for easy mowing, so that they don't appear to be running rampant. Second, meadow areas require some care to ensure that noxious weeds don't become established, although occasional spot cultivation or herbicide treatment won't take much time. Third, meadow areas must be visually interesting.

Depending on your local native plants, avoiding a weedy look might be achieved best by selective thinning, periodic cultivation, or occasional mowing or power-trimming of some parts of the meadow. Experimentation is in order. Each meadow area is unique; there is no single best management scheme. You'll probably be surprised by the diversity of beautiful native plants that care for themselves.

## Herbaceous Perennial Ground Covers

Once they have become established, several of the cultivated herbaceous perennial ground covers don't need much more maintenance than do native plants, provided that a good stand has been achieved. Where there are gaps in the canopy, you'll probably need to use mulch, herbicides, or cultivation to control weeds. Most of the commonly used species grow more uniformly if they are pruned back annually. Spring-flowering plants should be pruned when they have finished blooming. Summer- and fall-flowering plants should be pruned in the spring. Tops of plants that die back in the winter can be removed in late fall or early in the spring.

Pruning isn't essential. If you do decide to prune, never remove more than a third of the stems. The quickest way to prune is with a lawn mower elevated to the appropriate height by wheel extensions. You can catch the clippings in a bag attachment to be used as compost, mulch, or for off-site disposal. (Use a raised lawn mower with *extreme* care: Make sure you don't risk injury by sticking your foot under the raised deck.)

## Shrub and Vine Ground Covers

Several shrubs and vines suitable as ground covers require even less care after establishment than do the herbaceous perennial ground covers: They rarely need pruning. Unfortunately, shrubs and vines generally cost much more than herbaceous perennials, and they tend to spread more slowly, too. However, shrubs typically can be planted farther apart than herbaceous perennials.

## Ground Cover Spacing

Most of the common nongrass ground covers are best established from transplants purchased from a nursery. Nursery-grown plants are available, ready for planting, in containers ranging in size from 3 inches to gallon-sized pots, and they usually become established quicker than home-propagated plants.

The table (right) shows how large an area will be covered by 100 plants set various distances apart. Plant spacing depends on how quickly a particular species spreads, but a spacing of approximately 12 inches between plants is appropriate for many species.

## Planting Distances for 100 Plants

The distance between plantings of ground cover transplants or sod pieces determines how large an area will eventually be covered when the plants mature.

| Planting Distance (inches) | Area Covered (square feet) |
|---|---|
| 4 | 11 |
| 6 | 25 |
| 8 | 44 |
| 10 | 70 |
| 12 | 100 |
| 18 | 225 |
| 24 | 400 |
| 36 | 900 |
| 48 | 1600 |

*Although vines often grow and spread slowly, they make excellent ground covers, since they require little care after they become established.*

*Preparing the soil thoroughly before you plant ground covers will result in healthier plants and lower ongoing maintenance.*

## PREPARING THE SITE

Many nongrass ground cover plants are frequently used on very poorly prepared sites. However, they, too, will look better with less care if the growing conditions are nearly optimal. Spending extra time and money on site preparation at the outset will save you time, and perhaps money, later.

Newly developed areas and areas where grass will be replaced by lower-care plants need intensive preparation. Completely remove the old plants, eliminate as many weeds and weed seeds as possible, install drainage tile if the site tends to be wet, and incorporate fertilizers and organic matter to improve soil tilth.

### Clearing the Ground

The best time to start preparing for new plantings is early in the growing season. If you need to get rid of unwanted grass, apply glyphosate herbicide and then rent a sod cutter or hire professionals to cut and remove the sod. If you're landscaping a previously undeveloped site, mow off any existing vegetation and till it in. Once the soil is bare, allow weeds to sprout and grow a few inches, then apply glyphosate again, and wait at least a week before tilling. You can repeat this procedure once or twice.

Now is the time to install a drainage system if one is needed and to install permanent irrigation lines. (More details are given later in this chapter.)

### Improving the Soil

The next step is to amend the soil. Both sandy soils, which have poor aeration, and clay soils, which have poor water and nutrient retention, can be improved by adding a 2-inch layer of peat moss (about 3 cubic yards per 1,000 square feet) and tilling it in. Don't add sand to clay soil in an attempt to improve aeration—unless you add tremendous amounts of sand, you'll actually make aeration poorer. Fertilize and adjust pH on the basis of soil test results.

## RENOVATING GRASSED AREAS

Renovating grassed areas is much less costly and time consuming than installing new plantings, and it can sometimes significantly reduce maintenance needs. If you have a problem with thatch, for example, aerating the soil with a coring machine that removes soil plugs to a depth of more than 2 inches is a timesaving alternative to ongoing remedial treatments. You can tell that you have a thatch problem if you can't stick your finger down through the grass and easily touch the soil surface. A layer of matted organic material greater than about ½ inch is detrimental for most grasses. Thatch aggravates pest and disease infestations, it increases susceptibility to environmental stresses, and may lead to iron deficiency. Lawns with very thick thatch layers should be renovated or replaced.

Another technique that improves aeration is topdresssing the grass with about ½ inch of a weed-free compost, fine composted bark, or a blend of compost and sand. You can purchase bags of topdress mix blended for this purpose. You can also overseed with a better-adapted grass in places (an area under a tree in heavy shade, for example) where the existing grass isn't well suited.

### Installing Sod

Grass sod provides an instant lawn and can be installed almost any time during the growing season, provided the soil is moist. However, sodding is the most expensive way to establish grass. You'll almost certainly need professional assistance in laying it and, unfortunately, the lowest-maintenance varieties for your location may not be available as sod.

### Sowing Seed

You can sow grass seed yourself with either a handheld broadcast seeder or a push-type drop seeder. The latter is preferable because it tends to sow more uniformly and is easier to use. Be sure to seed at recommended rates. Too much seed can cause disease problems; too little can lead to excessive weed germination.

Cool-season grasses should be seeded in late summer and warm-season grasses in late spring or early summer. Warm-season grasses are often seeded slightly earlier on sites shaded by deciduous trees. This allows the grasses to start growing before the trees are in full leaf. After seeding, the soil should be rolled to provide firm contact with the seeds.

### Controlling Erosion

To control erosion and to encourage germination, apply a thin layer of straw (free of weed seeds) to the seedbed immediately after rolling it. Be sure to spread the straw thinly so that it doesn't prevent sunlight or water from reaching the soil. You can use other organic materials—including shredded bark, rice hulls, and wood shavings—instead of straw, but don't use sawdust. When temperatures are low, consider covering the area with clear polyethylene sheeting to speed germination. Applying these erosion-control methods by hand is easy on small areas; for large areas, use mechanized chopper/blowers. After application, water the soil until it is thoroughly moist. While the grass is becoming established, water it frequently and lightly. Avoid walking on the new grass until it is well established.

## CHOOSING LOW-CARE GROUND COVERS

Before you choose ground covers, study the chart (page 48) on the characteristics of some of the most widely used species. The information on plant spacing and maintenance needs will help you to estimate installation costs and

*If grassed areas cannot be easily or successfully renovated, installing sod is an alternative. However, sod can be expensive and you may need professional help to install it.*

# Ground Covers

| Name | Botanical Name | Plant Spacing | Characteristics | Maintenance |
|------|----------------|---------------|-----------------|-------------|
| Barrenworts | *Epimedium alpinum,* *E. grandiflorum, E. pinnatum* (Zones 4–8) | Space plants 9″–12″ apart | Herbaceous perennials to 12″ tall; maintain uniform height; dense foliage often lasting well into winter; white, yellow, or lavender flowers; adapted to semishade, most soils; often used under evergreens and shrubs | Remove oldest leaves in fall or early spring for best appearance |
| Bearberry | *Arctostaphylos uvaursi* (Zones 2–9) | Space plants 24″–30″ apart | Prostrate shrub to 6″–10″ tall; fine-textured broadleaf evergreen, with trailing stems, dark lustrous foliage, and bright red fruit; adapted to stony, sandy, and acid soils; particularly suited to sandy banks | Prune in early spring for denser branching |
| Bugleweed | *Ajuga reptans* (Zones 5–9) | Space plants 8″–12″ apart | Herbaceous perennial to 4″–8″ tall; creeper with blue or purple flowers; adapted to sun and shade, dry soils; a rapid grower; can be used alone or with other small plants | Susceptible to crown rot on wet sites, resulting in destruction of entire stands; aphids cause leaves to roll under at the edges (systemic insecticide needed for control) |
| Capeweed | *Phyla nodiflora* (Zones 9–10) | Space stolons or divisions 12″–14″ apart | Herbaceous perennial to 2″–4″ tall; creeper with greenish to purple leaves and light pink flowers; spreads rapidly; adapted to sun and shade, droughty soils; withstands trampling | Can be mowed like turfgrass |
| Coralberries | *Symphoricarpos orbiculatus* (Zones 3–9), *S. × chenaultii* (Zones 5–9) | Space plants 30″–36″ apart | Deciduous shrubs to 36″ tall; fine-textured foliage; spread rapidly by underground stems and form neat mats where a tall cover is acceptable; adapted to full sun and partial shade, poor soils | Prune in early spring for best appearance |
| Cotoneasters | *Cotoneaster adpressus* (Zones 5–9), *C. apiculatus* (Zones 5–9), *C. dammeri* (Zones 6–10), *C. microphyllus* (Zones 7–10) | Space plants about 36″ apart | Shrubs to 6″–30″ tall; flat, horizontally growing plants with bright red fruit; adapted to full sun; good for banks and in rough areas; self-seeding | Prune annually for best appearance; subject to fireblight, spider mite, and lace bug damage |
| Cowberry | *Vaccinium vitisidaea* (Zones 5–9) | Space plants about 12″ apart | Shrub to 12″ tall; evergreen with small pink flowers and dark red fruit; adapted to acid soils | Add organic matter to soil each fall; will not tolerate summer heat |
| Creeping lilyturf | *Liriope spicata* (Zones 5–10) | Space plants 8″–16″ apart | Herbaceous perennial to 12″ tall; grasslike evergreen with dark green leaves and purple flowers; forms a dense mat; adapted to full sun and full shade, most soils; tolerates salt spray | Susceptible to damage by slugs and snails |
| Creeping thyme | *Thymus serpyllum* (Zones 5–10) | Space plants 6″–10″ apart | Subshrub to 3″ tall; evergreen with purplish flowers; adapted to full sun, dry soils; often used as edging or between stepping stones | Susceptible to leaf blight in wet weather |
| Crownvetch | *Coronilla varia* (Zones 3–7) | Space plants 10″–14″ apart | Herbaceous perennial to 12″–24″ tall; small pink flowers; spreads by underground stems; adapted to neutral soils, but prefers slightly acidic soils; often used to cover dry, steep slopes | Mow in fall and dispose of clippings off site to avoid fire hazard and rodent habitat |

## Ground Covers (continued)

| Name | Botanical Name | Plant Spacing | Characteristics | Maintenance |
|---|---|---|---|---|
| Daylily | *Hemerocallis* species (Zones 3-10) | Space plants or divisions 18"-36" apart | Herbaceous perennials to 36" tall; bloom throughout the growing season; seldom bothered by diseases or insect pests; adapted to dry and boggy soils | Remove spent flower stalks for best appearance; occasional dividing can restore vigor |
| Dichondra | *Dichondra micrantha* (Zones 9-10) | Space clumps about 12" apart | Herbaceous perennial to 1"-2" tall; spreads rapidly by runners; adapted to sun and shade | Usually mowed like turfgrass; needs regular fertilizing for best appearance; avoid digging around the plants; poor drainage can result in alternaria root rot |
| Dwarf hollygrape | *Mahonia repens* (Zones 6-9) | Space plants 14"-18" apart | Shrub to 24" tall; rapidly growing, semievergreen, with yellow flowers; adapted to sun and shade, most soils | Prune in spring for best appearance |
| Dwarf lilyturf | *Ophiopogon japonicus* (Zones 7-10) | Space plants 8"-12" apart | Herbaceous perennial to 12" tall; lilylike, evergreen, with dark green leaves and purple flowers; forms a dense mat; adapted to full sun and full shade, most soils; tolerates salt spray | No special care needed |
| Dwarf polygonum | *Polygonum cuspidatum* var. *compactum* (Zones 4-10) | Space plants 12"-16" apart | Herbaceous perennial to 12-24" tall; deciduous, with red foliage in fall; spreads rapidly; adapted to full sun, rocky or gravelly soils | Mow off dead leaves in early spring |
| English ivy | *Hedera helix* (Zones 5-9) | Space plants 10"-14" apart | Vine to 6"-8" tall; evergreen coarse foliage; forms a dense cover; adapted to shade and full sun; often used where it can spread on the ground and climb adjacent walls | No special care needed |
| Germander | *Teucrium chamaedrys* (Zones 6-10) | Space plants 12"-18" apart | Shrub to 10" tall; adapted to sun and partial shade; often used as border for walks | Prune in early spring for best appearance; might need winter mulch where ground freezes |
| Goldmoss stonecrop | *Sedum acre* (Zones 4-10) | Space plants 8"-10" apart | Herbaceous perennial to 4" tall; spreads by creeping, forming mats of tiny leaves; adapted to dry soils; often used between stepping stones and in rocky places | Mow off spent flowers for best appearance; mow in spring to promote branching for thicker stand |
| Ground-ivy | *Glechoma hederacea* (Zones 3-9) | Space plants 12"-14" apart | Herbaceous perennial to 3" tall; spreads by creeping and forms low mats; adapted to sun and shade | Mow occasionally for more uniform appearance; considered a weed in grass, and can be troublesome if not confined |
| Heartleaf bergenia | *Bergenia cordifolia* (Zones 5-10) | Space plants 12"-15" apart | Perennial herb to 12" tall; creeping, clumpy thick foliage and pink flowers habit; adapted to sun and partial shade | Might need winter mulch in the North to reduce cold injury |
| Honeysuckle | *Lonicera japonica* (Zones 5-9) | Space plants 30"-42" apart | Vine to 4"-6" tall; evergreen to semievergreen foliage and fragrant flowers that are first white, then yellow; adapted to sun and partial shade | Prune heavily in early spring for best appearance; can be troublesome if allowed to get out of control (should be pruned annually) |

## Ground Covers (continued)

| Name | Botanical Name | Plant Spacing | Characteristics | Maintenance |
|---|---|---|---|---|
| Iceplants | *Cephalophyllum* species, *Carpobrotus* species, *Delosperma* species, *Drosanthemum* species, *Maleophora* species, *Lampranthus* species (Zone 10) | Space plants 6"–24" apart, depending on spreading rate of particular species | Herbaceous perennials to 3"–24" tall; evergreens, with brilliant flowers that open only in full sun; often used on banks and roadsides | No special care needed |
| Japanese holly | *Ilex crenata* (Zones 6–10) | Space plants 24"–48" apart | Shrub to 24" tall; evergreen; adapted to semishade; often used on small banks | Prune lightly in spring for best appearance; might need winter mulch in the North to reduce cold injury |
| Japanese spurge | *Pachysandra terminalis* (Zones 5–8) | Space plants 10"–16" apart | Subshrub to 6" tall; quickly spreading evergreen; spreads by underground stems; adapted to shade (leaves become yellowish in full sun) | No special care needed; often called the ideal ground cover (at least for shaded areas); sometimes attacked by scale insects |
| Junipers | *Juniperus horizontalis* (Zones 3–9), *J. sabina* (Zones 3–9), *J. procumbens* (Zones 4–9), *J. chinensis* (Zones 4–10), *J. conferta* (Zones 4–10) | Space plants 30"–48" apart, depending on spread of particular species | Shrubs to 12"–24" tall; forms vary from low and spreading to upright; foliage varies from light green to steel blue (often purple in winter); adapted to sun, dry soils | Low-growing forms need little or no pruning |
| Memorial rose | *Rosa wichuraiana* (Zones 5–9) | Space plants about 48" apart | Shrub to 6"–12" tall; trailing semievergreen, with 2-inch white flowers; adapted to droughty soils; tolerates salt spray; stems root wherever they touch soil | Prune out diseased shoots regularly |
| Moss sandwort | *Arenaria verna* (Zones 2–9) | Space plants 12"–16" apart | Herbaceous perennial to 3" tall; mossy; adapted to moist partial shade, fertile soils; often used between flagstones; self-seeds and can become weedy | Mow off flowers to prevent self-seeding; some winter protection needed on cold, exposed sites |
| Periwinkles | *Vinca major*, *V. minor* (Zones 5–10) | Space plants 10"–14" apart | Vinelike subshrubs to 8" tall; trailing evergreens, with dark green leaves and purple, blue, or white flowers; *V. minor* has small leaves, *V. major* has large leaves; adapted to full sun and partial shade, well-drained soils; often used on rocky banks | Mow in early spring for best appearance |
| St. Johnswort | *Hypericum calycinum* (Zones 6–10) | Space plants 30"–36" apart | Shrub to 9"–12" tall; semievergreen; bright yellow flowers from midsummer until frost and red leaves in fall; adapted to semishade, sandy soils | Mow in early spring for best appearance |
| Sand strawberry | *Fragaria chiloensis* (Zones 6–10) | Space plants 12"–18" apart | Herbaceous perennial to 6" tall; spreads rapidly; similar in appearance to strawberry species cultivated for fruit; adapted to most soils, especially sandy soils | Mow in early spring for best appearance |

*South African daisy* (Gazania rigens)

## Ground Covers (continued)

| Name | Botanical Name | Plant Spacing | Characteristics | Maintenance |
|------|----------------|---------------|-----------------|-------------|
| South African daisy | *Gazania rigens* (Zones 9-10) | Space plants 10″-14″ apart | Herbaceous perennial to 6″-9″ tall; light green foliage; orange flowers bloom continuously during spring and summer; adapted to well-drained soils; tolerates drought; no serious pests or diseases | Mow after blooming for best appearance |
| Strawberry geranium | *Saxifraga stolonifera* (Zones 7-9) | Space plants 12″-18″ apart | Herbaceous perennial to 15″ tall; spreads by runners; adapted to partial shade, heavy soils | No special care needed |
| Weeping lantanas | *Lantana sellowiana* *L. montevidensis* (Zones 8-10) | Space plants 36″-48″ apart | Shrubs with trailing branches to 36″ long; adapted to sun, most soils; tolerates salt; often mixed with junipers or used as a hanging cover for walls | Prune heavily in early spring to prevent formation of dead centers |
| Winter-creeper | *Euonymus fortunei* (Zones 5-10) | Space plants 12″-16″ apart | Trailing vine to 36″ long, depending on cultivar; evergreen, with uniform leaves and rapid, almost flat growth | Mow in early spring for best appearance; scale insects can be serious pests |
| Wintergreen | *Gaultheria procumbens* (Zones 5-7) | Space plants 12″-18″ apart | Subshrub to 4″ tall; evergreen creeper; adapted to moist shade, acid soils | Mow occasionally for best appearance |

will guide you in selecting low-care species. Before making final decisions, it would still be a good idea to ask your local nursery staff to recommend the most suitable species and varieties for your location. You'll probably find that your choices are limited by which species are available locally.

## PLANTING NONGRASS GROUND COVERS

In most areas, spring is the best time for planting nongrass ground cover plants. Fall is also a good time in areas not subject to severe winters. If the ground is too uneven or steep to till the entire area, dig individual planting holes and mix peat moss or other organic material with the soil from each hole.

The plants should be set at the recommended spacing, in either square or triangular formation, and at the same level at which they were growing before transplanting. Pack soil firmly around the roots, and leave a slight basin around the stem to hold water. Water thoroughly after planting, and irrigate as necessary during the remainder of the first growing season (1 to 2 inches of water each week).

Probably the best temporary mulch to use for establishing nongrass ground cover plants is black plastic sheeting weighted down and with holes cut for the plants. Cover the plastic with a decorative mulch if you desire, and remember to hand-weed around the young plants. When the plants have covered a large proportion of the area, replace the plastic mulch with an organic or nonorganic particle mulch.

## MAINTAINING LAWNS

If your easy-care landscape includes even a small grassed area, you'll want to get the routine lawn chores out of the way as quickly as possible. There is no need to feel guilty about cutting back on lawn maintenance; in some cases, too much care can actually lead to more maintenance in the long run. For instance, both mowing too low and too frequently and removing the grass clippings can result in very unhealthy grass.

### Mowing

The most important effect of mowing takes place underground; the leaf area of a grass plant directly affects its root development. In general, grass mowed higher will have more extensive roots, be capable of better nutrient uptake, be more drought tolerant, and have extra food storage. Well-developed root systems are essential for healthy stress-resistant plants. If you want grass that thrives on as little water as possible and shrugs off pest and disease attacks, avoid mowing too low.

**Mowing height** The ideal mowing height depends on the grass species, the season, and the location, but there is a general rule to go by for most cool-season (northern) grasses: Don't clip off more than a third of the blade height. Preferably, clip less and as high as possible without the blades bending over while mowing. High-cut grass actually grows more slowly than low-cut grass, because of self-shading, so you'll need to mow high-cut grass less often. Also, the extra shade under high-cut grass will tend to reduce possible weed seed germination.

Some warm-season grasses, such as the Bermudagrasses, should be mowed relatively low, between 1 and 2 inches. Remember, mowing is always a shock to grass; it suddenly has much less capability for making food, especially when the grass is growing slowly. During slow-growth periods, clip off less of each blade than usual.

**Mowing frequency** Grass health is also adversely affected by too-frequent mowing. Root growth and spreading rate tend to be slowed by mowing more frequently than about once a week, regardless of mowing height. So give your grass a few days to recover before you mow again—you'll save time and have a healthier lawn. However, too-infrequent mowing tends to increase thatch. In many areas, mowing every 7 to 10 days is best.

**Grass clippings** Even with a mower that has a catcher, removing grass clippings takes time (for bagging) and money (for bags). It also wastes plant nutrients, especially nitrogen. Leaving clippings in place does no harm, provided that the clippings aren't so long that they clump and form mats, and grass clippings do not contribute to thatch buildup. If you're leaving clippings where they fall, the best time to mow is when the grass is dry; the clippings won't tend to clump and mat so much.

**Mower Types**

If you find clippings aesthetically objectionable, consider buying a mulching mower, which chops up clippings very fine before dropping them. Using a mulching mower will have the

same effect on grass quality as a conventional mower without a clipping catcher.

Reel mowers are best suited to manicured lawns that are nearly flat and not very large. Rotary mowers are significantly faster, and they're much less likely to scalp grass on an uneven terrain. For really rough terrain, reciprocating-blade mowers are most appropriate—

*Improper mowing of a lawn can cause scalping.*

## Mowing Heights

L awns are better able to resist weeds, disease, and insects if mowed at the correct height. When grass grows ⅛ to ½ times over the recommended height it is time to mow it.

| Grass | Height in Inches |
|---|---|
| Bahiagrass | 2–3 |
| Bentgrass | ¼–1 |
| Bermudagrass | |
|   Common | ¾–1½ |
|   Improved | ½–1 |
| Bluegrass | |
|   Common | 2–3 |
|   Improved | 1½–2½ |
|   Rough | 1–2 |
| Buffalograss | 1½–2 |
| Carpetgrass | 1–2 |
| Centipedegrass | 1–2 |
| Dichondra | ½–1½ |
| Fescue | |
|   Chewings, hard | 1–2½ |
|   Red | 1½–2½ |
|   Tall | 2–3 |
| Annual ryegrass | 1½–2 |
| Perennial ryegrass | 1–2 |
| St. Augustine grass | 2–3 |
| Zoysiagrass | 1–2 |

some of them can cut through woody stems up to ½ inch thick. To save time, use a gasoline-powered mower instead of an electric one—that way, you won't need to worry about slicing the cord.

## Mower Maintenance

Gasoline-powered mowers have only a few maintenance requirements; if you satisfy them you should be able to avoid major repairs for years. Most important is to use fresh gasoline. Unless you want to head straight for the shop next spring, never fail to drain the gasoline from the tank (and from the carburetor bowl on some mowers) after the end of the mowing season. Check to make sure that the oil level is correct before you begin mowing, and keep the air filter element clean.

Keep your mower's blade(s) sharp and you won't have to slow down for very thick grass. Grass blade tips torn by dull mower blades are susceptible to pests and diseases, and cleanly sliced grass looks much better, at least up close, than torn grass. Plan your mowing so clippings don't end up where you'll have to rake them—if you have a side-discharge mower, keep the discharge side away from paved areas. Use a different mowing pattern each time you mow, or at least alternate among a few patterns, to avoid grooved tire tracks and too many clippings in the same spots. Clean the underside of your rotary mower frequently, so it lifts the grass up and cuts evenly. And always play it safe when mowing—a trip to the hospital will cost you more than just time!

## RAKING

The best way to reduce the time you spend raking leaves is to avoid planting trees that produce a lot of large leaves that decompose slowly. Look at your neighbors' yards in the fall to see which kinds of trees cause most problems with dropped leaves. Don't plant those kinds. If your site already has one or more of the worst offenders, use debris-swallowing ground cover plants beneath the trees. Still, some leaves, if only from the trees down the block, probably will end up on your grassed areas. If they aren't piled deeply enough to block the light reaching the lawn, they shouldn't harm the grass—you don't have to remove them.

Heavy leaf accumulations can be removed faster with vacuuming or blowing equipment,

*Top and opposite: Gasoline-powered mowers save time. The choice between a riding mower and a push-type mower should depend on the size of the lawn. Bottom: A lightweight rectangular frame designed to hold plastic leaf bags makes collecting leaves much easier.*

*Top: Using different patterns each time you mow will prevent grooved tire tracks from forming.*
*Bottom: A powered string trimmer quickly cuts grass that is difficult to reach.*

but a handrake is adequate for cleaning up small areas. Use a wide rake that covers a lot of ground in a hurry. To save time bagging the leaves, purchase a lightweight rectangular frame that's sized to fit around the tops of plastic leaf bags and hold them open. This inexpensive device makes one-person leaf raking and disposal much easier.

## TRIMMING AND EDGING

In a well-designed easy-care landscape, the need for hand-trimming and edging is kept to a minimum with boundaries that care for themselves. There are two main types of low-care boundaries. One type uses hardscape materials or mulch to provide buffer zones between different kinds of plants (for example, mulched areas surrounding trees, separating the tree trunks from grass). The other uses plants that naturally establish fairly precise lines of demarcation between themselves and other kinds of plants (for example, prostrate shrub ground covers against backdrops of upright shrubs). Boundaries that tend to become ragged without periodic maintenance should be avoided; examples are borders between grass and raised curbs and grass around tree trunks.

Edges of hardscape features adjoining grassed areas should be placed flush with the ground to make mowing easier and to make hand-edging unnecessary. Use mulch or non-grass ground cover plants around trees to avoid hand-trimming. Powered string trimmers and brush cutters are useful time-savers for hard-to-mow areas, especially around curbs and other hardscape features that extend above ground level. To avoid plant damage, never use them around woody plants.

Edgers, whether manual or powered, won't get much use in a self-maintaining landscape. You'll probably find it sufficient to own an inexpensive manual edger and to rent a powered edger very occasionally, if at all.

## WATERING

Some grasses and ground covers use much more water than others. In general, cool-season (northern) grasses tend to use more water than warm-season (southern) grasses. By choosing grasses or ground covers with low water-use rates, you might be able to get by with very little supplementary watering—depending, of course, on your climate. However, don't plant a grass or ground cover unsuited to your site just because it conserves water.

Another way to reduce the water needs of lawns and ground covers (as well as other plants), and hence the time required for irrigation chores, is to shield the plants from drying winds. For quick results and long-term low maintenance, solid fencing and constructed screens are best. Of course, low-care tree and

shrub species and cultivars, discussed in the next chapter, need less water than other trees and shrubs.

## Automatic Irrigation

To eliminate the chore of watering even a small area by hand, consider a permanent irrigation system that does the job automatically. For large lawns or ground cover areas, buried drip, or trickle, irrigation systems are unwieldy because each emitter provides water over only a few square feet—you would need to install a large number of emitters. Drip systems are appropriate for very small lawn areas and also for areas with nongrass ground cover plants, where one emitter can serve several plants that are spaced about a foot apart. If drip irrigation makes sense for your site, see the information about such systems in the chapter on vegetable gardening (page 99).

**Sprinkler systems**   For watering large areas of ground cover, sprinkler systems are the best choice. They spread the water evenly over the entire lawn, which allows more economical use of water. If a timer is used, all the watering can be done at night, when evaporation is minimal.

**Design and installation of the sprinkler systems**   You can hire professionals to install a sprinkler system, or you can do it yourself. Modern plastic materials make installation easy. Some manufacturers and retailers of sprinkler components even provide design services free or at nominal cost.

---

### Water-Use Rates
(lowest to highest)

| Cool-Season Grasses | Warm-Season Grasses |
|---|---|
| Fine fescues | Bermudagrass hybrids |
| Perennial ryegrass | Centipedegrass |
| Tall fescue | Zoysiagrass |
| Creeping bentgrass | Bahiagrass |
| Kentucky bluegrass | St. Augustine grass |

---

*Sprinkler systems should distribute water evenly over an entire area to avoid creating spots that are too wet or too dry.*

*Overlapping sprinkler patterns provide the most even coverage.*

**Sprinkler coverage** The most important timesaving consideration in designing and installing a sprinkler system is proper coverage. Unless you can arrange it so that all parts of the area receive the same amount of water, you'll have to overwater some areas in order to properly water the areas that receive less. Of course, some areas may need significantly more or less water because of shading or soil differences.

Both nonrotating and rotating sprinkler heads can provide coverage throughout whole, half-, or quarter-circles. High winds distort spray patterns; if winds are likely to be a problem at your site, use closely spaced heads with small coverage patterns. If possible, water at night when there is less wind.

### Automatic Irrigation Schedulers

Automatic irrigation schedulers are great timesavers, especially in arid areas. In areas with highly variable rainfall, a manual override is necessary. Automatic irrigation schedulers that use a timer are better suited to residential use than are the schedulers that use moisture readings, because the former tend to be more durable and allow more flexibility. Reliable timer schedulers are readily available from $50 to $200. The more costly models are needed to cover larger areas.

## FERTILIZING

Heavy applications of high-nitrogen fertilizers produce grass of luxuriant deep green. They also cause undesirably lush growth, which means more frequent mowing and possible thatch buildup. Only use enough nitrogen to keep the lawn green and healthy.

Trials have shown that adding up to 8 pounds of potassium per 1,000 square feet per year, even to soil already high in potassium, improves wear tolerance. Potassium also increases resistance to many lawn diseases.

Phosphorus, the third major plant nutrient, is primarily needed in areas that receive lots of rainfall.

The easiest way to apply lawn nutrients is with balanced lawn fertilizers that apply all three nutrients. These are available as soluble fertilizers in both dry and liquid form, or as slow-release fertilizers. Soluble fertilizers must be applied from three to eight times a year, depending on the type of fertilizer and the length of your growing season. Slow-release fertilizers, however, can be applied once or twice a year.

There are two kinds of slow-release fertilizers: organic and stabilized inorganic. Both kinds are more expensive than soluble fertilizers, but since they release nitrogen and other nutrients slowly over time, a whole year's dose can be applied at once without fear of damage to foliage. Organic slow-release fertilizers include plant and animal by-products such as manure, activated sewage sludge, and cottonseed meal. They tend to be bulky and difficult to spread evenly, but they contain organic matter that benefits the lawn.

The most common stabilized inorganic slow-release fertilizers are easy-to-handle granules with coatings or formulations designed to release soluble nutrients slowly. Unfortunately, these fertilizers are expensive compared with soluble fertilizers and many of the organic slow-release fertilizers. When purchasing fertilizers, base your price comparisons on the percentage of nutrients per pound and ask garden store staff how much of each kind must be applied and how frequently.

## WEEDING

Established grass can't be mulched for weed control, but many of the nongrass ground cover plants can be. In contrast, herbicides are usually quite effective for controlling weeds in grass, but it can be difficult or even impossible to find suitable herbicides for some other ground cover plants. An exception is glyphosate, which you can spot-apply to weeds if you are very careful not to let it contact the ground cover plants—a tedious chore, at best.

Thus, the best weed management choices in terms of low maintenance are herbicides for grass and mulch for nongrasses. You can also weed by hand, but this takes so much time that it's really suited to only very small areas.

### Weeding With Herbicides

There are two categories of herbicides: preemergence and postemergence. Preemergence herbicides are applied to the soil before weed seeds germinate. Postemergence herbicides are applied to actively growing weeds.

Apply preemergence herbicides in the spring, before weeds emerge or after they have been removed. Preemergence herbicides are highly selective: They destroy the seeds of

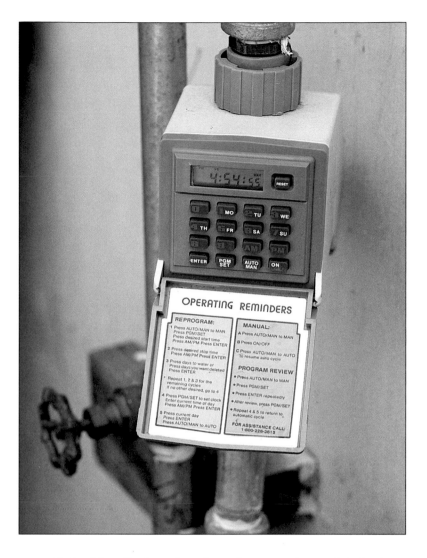

*Automatic irrigation schedulers are convenient and relatively inexpensive devices, and they can save you considerable time in lawn care.*

many kinds of broadleaf weeds and weedy annual grasses but spare established perennial grasses. Most preemergence herbicides can be applied easily to grassed areas with a hose-end sprayer or a small pressure sprayer. Some preemergence herbicides are granulated and can be applied with a fertilizer spreader.

After broadleaf weeds have germinated, they can most easily be controlled by spraying the entire lawn with a selective herbicide such as 2,4-D. To control grassy weeds, you should spot-spray with a nonselective herbicide, such as glyphosate.

### Mulching to Control Weeds

Mulch will control nearly all weeds in nongrass ground cover areas. Probably the best long-term mulching materials for these areas are organic particles (shredded bark, bark chips, straw). Plastic or other types of sheet mulch, such as cardboard, won't allow the ground cover plants to spread as they should.

# Low-Care Woody Ornamentals

*There are some woody ornamentals that require very little care. In fact, they are among the most self-maintaining of any of the plants you might add to your low-care garden.*

Y ou can't just plant and forget woody ornamentals, but assuming that you've chosen appropriate species and cultivars, done a reasonable planting job, and provided a bit of training to those that require it, you certainly won't need to pamper your trees, shrubs, and vines. Yet, there are other low-maintenance considerations besides how much care these plants need. The larger ones, at least, are going to have an influence on the maintenance needs of the site for a long time to come.

*A massed planting of various evergreens combined with hardscape features such as walkways and stone walls make a distinctive low-care landscape.*

*Since a woody ornamental will change its form and size over the years, consider future, rather than current, conditions as you decide where to place it in a low-care landscape.*

## SETTING GOALS

Unlike ground covers, which soon reach their full spread, woody ornamentals change their form and size throughout their lifetime. As woody plants mature they change the garden environment by providing shade, shelter from wind, competition for water and nutrients, and visual screening. Consequently, you need to consider the impact your woody plants will have on other landscape features, which means relating your goals for a low-care landscape primarily to future conditions in your landscape, rather than to current conditions. Remember, a maple tree will remain under 10

feet for only a few years, but it might top 40 feet for dozens of years.

Beds of woody ornamentals have very flexible roles in low-maintenance landscapes. They can be more or less easy care, depending mainly on your desire for formality. Since trees and shrubs are subject to the vagaries of the elements over long periods of time, only rarely do they maintain perfectly symmetrical shapes—unless you train them. A perfect lawn requires much work; a row of perfect trees with precisely matching forms requires too much work. To save maintenance time on woody ornamentals, you must be willing to

## Low-Care Trees, Shrubs, and Vines

| Name | Botanical Name | Characteristics |
|---|---|---|
| **Low-Care Large Trees** | | |
| American beech | *Fagus grandifolia* | Prune off low branches when young |
| Austrian pine | *Pinus nigra* | Good form, disease problems in Northeast |
| Balsam fir | *Abies balsamea* | |
| Black gum | *Nyssa sylvatica* | Produces little litter |
| Canada hemlock | *Tsuga canadensis* | |
| Chestnut oak | *Quercus muehlenbergii* | Especially desirable for planting in clumps |
| Norway spruce | *Picea abies* | |
| Paper birch | *Betula papyrifera* | For the North only |
| Red maple | *Acer rubrum* | Especially desirable for planting in clumps |
| Red oak | *Quercus rubra* | Especially desirable for planting in clumps |
| Serbian spruce | *Picea omorika* | |
| Sugar maple | *Acer saccharum* | |
| White birch | *Betula pendula* | |
| White oak | *Quercus alba* | |
| **Low-Care Small Trees and Shrubs** | | |
| Arrowwoods | *Viburnum* species | |
| Crabapples (disease-resistant cultivars only) | *Malus* species | |
| Gumi | *Elaeagnus multiflora* | |
| Hawthorns | *Crataegus* species | Extremely hardy |
| Juneberries | *Amelanchier* species | |
| Kousa | *Cornus kousa* | |
| Siberian peashrub | *Caragana arborescens* | Disease resistant |
| Sourwood | *Oxydendrum arboreum* | Extremely hardy |
| Yews | *Taxus* species | |
| Yuccas | *Yucca* species | |
| **Low-Care Vines** | | |
| Boston ivy | *Parthenocissus tricuspidata* | |
| Five-leaf akebia | *Akebia quinata* | Good for covering chain-link fencing; somewhat invasive |
| Trumpet creeper | *Campsis radicans* | Very hardy |
| Virginia creeper | *Parthenocissus quinquefolia* | |

accept the imperfections invariably associated with them.

## PLANNING AREAS OF WOODY ORNAMENTALS

Which trees, shrubs, and vines will require the least maintenance at your site? First, look around your neighborhood to see which woody plants, cultivated or growing wild, are doing well with little or no attention. If a plant is thriving with minimal care nearby, chances are that it would thrive with minimal care in your yard. This approach is like planting weeds—they might not be spectacular, but they're easy to grow!

What if you aren't satisfied with the commonplace? Search for more exotic low-care species and cultivars, keeping in mind that exceptionally adaptable plants (those that are most tolerant of climatic extremes, poor soil conditions, excessive competition, and pest or disease infestations) are the most promising candidates for self-maintaining landscapes. Moreover, don't forget that easy-care woody plants must be maintenance-compatible with neighboring plants.

The accompanying chart lists some woody plants suited to low-maintenance landscapes.

## CHOOSING LOW-CARE WOODY ORNAMENTALS

Don't assume that your choice of plants must be limited to species and varieties available locally. If some of the easy-care plants you

*When planting an ornamental prepare a hole that is shallow rather than deep and at least 18 to 24 inches wider than the rootball.*

want aren't available from nearby nurseries, ask whether they can be ordered or contact mail-order specialty nurseries.

To lower costs, most mail-order plants are shipped bare-root (with no soil around the roots) when they are dormant. Plants purchased locally may be bare-root, balled-and-burlapped (with a soil ball around the roots), or containerized (in pots). Any of these is acceptable if the plants are dormant, but you should not buy bare-root plants that are in leaf. You can plant balled-and-burlapped or containerized woody ornamentals at any time during the growing season if you're careful to see that they get ample water, but they are likely to do best if you plant them in early spring or late fall.

Be cautious about trying unusual trees, shrubs, or vines—you don't want to have to remove or relocate them when you discover that they don't perform as you expected. To avoid such problems, try to learn as much as you can about exotic species and varieties before you plant them. Unfortunately, some nursery catalogs exaggerate the niceties of some of the plants they sell, so get a second opinion before you order a miracle plant.

## Using Computer Programs to Choose Plants

Several computer programs (page 108) are now available to help you choose woody ornamentals. These programs provide easily accessed information on the characteristics and cultural requirements of dozens, and in some cases hundreds, of plants. One or more of your local nurseries probably offer computer-aided landscape design services, or perhaps your extension office has a landscaping program that you can use. Ferreting information from books and catalogs takes much more time than using a computer database.

## PLANTING

Within the past decade, a new technology for establishing landscape plants has been developed by horticulturists. Here are some recommendations, based on their work, for planting balled-and-burlapped and bare-root trees and shrubs. Most of these recommendations are at odds with traditional advice, yet they can save you both time and money.

## Digging a Large Planting Hole

The proponents of the new technology and the traditionalists agree on one thing: A large planting hole is desirable—at least 18 inches to 24 inches bigger than the rootball. Here, *bigger* means wider, not deeper. Except in dry soil, a slightly shallow hole is better than one that is too deep. A shallow hole avoids the problem of settling, which can cause poor root aeration, slow growth, and impaired stress resistance.

## Handling the Roots

Balled-and-burlapped plants should have the burlap removed from the sides of their rootballs after they are placed in the holes. Don't worry about removing the burlap on the bottom: Unless it is plastic instead of real burlap, it won't interfere with root growth. Bare-root plants should have their roots exposed to the air for as short a time as possible. Growing root ends can be damaged if they become dry. They can also be damaged by high temperatures, so keep plants out of the sun until you are ready to place them in their holes.

Some balled-and-burlapped plants have their rootballs supported by wire baskets. Remove the baskets so that they don't interfere with root growth. To prevent eventual strangulation, remove all string and rope from around stems and roots.

Never attempt to twist large roots around to fit an undersized hole. If you can't take the time to enlarge the hole, it's better to prune the roots than to twist them. Prune any roots that are kinked or circling other roots.

## Fertilizing the Backfill

Add some soluble fertilizer to the backfill soil to give the plant a quick start. An alternative that can delay the need to fertilize again for up to a year is to add slow-release fertilizer tablets. Place the tablets no more than about 3 inches below the soil surface, or the feeder roots won't benefit from the fertilizer.

## Controlling Weeds

Weed control is a necessity in newly planted beds. Heavy mulching works well, but keep the mulch away from the base of the plants to avoid bark suffocation and rodent damage. Placing solid plastic sheeting under the mulch can restrict aeration of the roots. Perforated

sheeting is a better choice, or use organic or inorganic mulch materials without plastic underneath. Limestone gravel is not a suitable mulch; it tends to increase soil pH, which causes chlorosis (leaf yellowing) of several woody species. To avoid inhibiting root growth, limit mulch depth to about 4 inches to allow adequate root aeration. There is such a thing as too much mulch!

## Pruning and Staking

Assuming that sufficient water for good growth will be available throughout the first growing season, don't prune the tops of newly transplanted trees and shrubs, except to remove damaged branches or to start training the plants. Pruning reduces the plant's leaf area and, consequently, its rate of growth. The traditional notion is to prune to bring the top into balance with the roots. Faster growth is more important.

Staking produces weak trees that are unable to support themselves well. If you feel that you must stake a plant, do it loosely, so the plant has some freedom of movement. Young trees that are allowed to bend with the wind develop much more trunk strength than rigidly staked trees.

*To make it easier to plant a balled-and-burlapped plant, the burlap need be removed only from the sides of the rootball; burlap left on the bottom of the rootball won't inhibit root growth.*

*Slow-release fertilizer tablets placed about 3 inches below the soil surface can delay the need to fertilize again for up to one year.*

### Planting in Herbicide-Treated Sod

Fruit trees planted in herbicide-treated sod grow faster than trees planted in untreated sod or in bare soil kept weed-free with herbicides or cultivation. The treated sod provides a mulch that moderates soil temperatures, leaves pores for aeration and water filtration as the grass roots decompose, and provides slowly released nutrients to the trees. Planting in herbicide-treated sod is much easier than digging out the sod and applying imported mulch, and it should be effective for ornamental trees and shrubs as well as for any fruit trees.

## FERTILIZING

Some of the traditional recommendations for fertilizing trees and shrubs are inappropriate, expensive, and time consuming. For example, placing N-P-K fertilizer in deep holes underneath a tree's canopy is extremely inefficient. This is because the feeder roots of typical woody plants are concentrated in the top few inches of the soil and extend far beyond their canopies. Just broadcast the fertilizer and water it in thoroughly.

### Broadcasting Fertilizer

The most significant nutrient influencing the growth of woody ornamentals is nitrogen. Many soils have more than enough phosphorus and potassium for enhanced tree and shrub growth provided that nitrogen is added. According to tests, broadcasting high-nitrogen soluble or slow-release fertilizers (or complete fertilizers for soils deficient in potassium or phosphorus) over the surface of a plant's entire root zone is at least as effective as more time-consuming techniques. Time-consuming techniques to be avoided include deep fertilizing, foliar feeding, and fertilizing the plant by injection.

### Using the Right Amount of Fertilizer

How much fertilizer should be applied? Recommendations based on trunk diameter are confusing when applied to shrubs and tend to result in underfertilization of large trees. It makes better sense to apply a constant rate of nitrogen (and equivalent or somewhat lower rates of potassium or phosphorus for soil that is deficient in either of those nutrients) per unit area within the root zone.

For trees and shrubs, annual broadcast applications of about ½ pound of nitrogen per 100 square feet are appropriate. If the root systems of two or more trees overlap, don't increase the application rate in the overlap areas or in areas where grass, ground covers, or other understory plants are within the root zones of trees and shrubs. To avoid burning herbaceous plants, you should split annual applications of soluble fertilizer into two or three separate doses, spaced at least a month apart. Watering-in soluble fertilizer immediately after you've applied it will also help to prevent burning. A good time to apply fertilizer is in the early spring, then ample nutrients are available throughout the growing season.

## MULCHING

Mulching woody plants will enhance the efficiency of your fertilizer applications. The density of feeder roots is significantly higher under mulch than under grass or bare soil. This means that more of the fertilizer you apply to mulched trees will be taken up by the trees, since those trees have the greatest number of feeder roots. Of course, mulching also prevents nutrients from being stolen from woody plants by grass and weeds. Thus, if you don't want to waste fertilizer, mulch your trees and shrubs.

Assuming that you have grouped trees and shrubs into mulched beds, the need for debris disposal work should be minimal. Dropped leaves, twigs, and fruits will simply add to the mulch layer, and they won't be unsightly unless you use a light-colored particle mulch, such as gravel, or a sheet mulch (white plastic is worst). The ideal mulch for hiding litter is composed of dark brown organic particles, such as bark nuggets.

You'll need to renew organic mulch only rarely if you put black plastic sheeting under it. Use perforated plastic (available from garden centers) to allow air and water to reach plant roots. Also, you'll have fewer weeds making it through the mulch if you install a layer of plastic sheeting.

The main drawback of mulch is the risk of rodent damage to plants. Voles can severely damage or even kill small trees by girdling them. Aside, perhaps, from traps and poison, the most effective control is to keep mulch well back from the base of trees and shrubs, which means you will need to hand-weed or use herbicide around the trunks. Ask your local extension agent about the most appropriate management techniques for rodents in your area.

## MANAGING PESTS AND DISEASES

Failing to treat pest or disease infestations immediately almost invariably results in extra time in the long run. Delaying action might mean that you'll need to spray a larger area or to spray more times. When you see significant plant damage, immediately seek expert advice on what steps, if any, you should take.

### Systemic Pesticides

Various systemic pesticides are registered for use on ornamental trees and shrubs. Once applied, by foliar spray, soil drench, or injection, these pesticides move throughout the plants to provide long-lasting protection that can't be washed off by rain. Systemic pesticides save time and trouble. They're quicker and easier to apply than conventional contact pesticides. In addition, they need fewer reapplications.

Systemic pesticides capable of controlling a broad spectrum of tree and shrub pests are available. In the future also look for systemic pesticides derived from the tropical tree

known as neem. Neem-based pesticides have very low toxicity for humans, yet they are quite potent against over one hundred kinds of insect pests.

### Horticultural Oil

Horticultural oil will save you time in three ways. It has extremely low toxicity for people, so you don't need to be as fastidious about protection during spraying or cleanup. It has a long shelf life and is easy to store, so you

*Mulch composed of dark brown organic particles not only prevents weeds from stealing the nutrients in the soil but also hides any organic litter, such as leaves, twigs, and conifer needles.*

*Pruning a hedge into strict formal shapes can be a time-consuming task. Simple, less tailored shapes, the low-care alternative, are often just as pleasing.*

can buy a big bottle and keep it for a long time without worrying about it degrading. Also, it is effective against a wide range of pests, so you can use it to replace a set of several pesticides with more limited effectiveness and different application instructions.

## TRAINING AND PRUNING

If you're unexcited by the prospect of spending hours on training and pruning, remember these two rules when you're selecting woody ornamentals: Use as many conifers as possible, and use conifers that are the right size. Unless they outgrow their allotted space or the plants are damaged, most conifers require little or no pruning. Of course, you can shear and clip conifers to formal shapes, but to do that well takes considerable time.

### Shaping Evergreen Shrubs

If you decide to shape your evergreen shrubs or have already shaped them, don't shear them.

The result is often an unnatural appearance with dense growth at the branch ends, which prevents light from reaching the center of the plants. The low-maintenance method for training evergreens is to prune new growth by hand, close to side branches or outward-facing buds. Although it takes more time initially to prune this way, the shrubs will keep a more natural shape and need far less frequent pruning to look well tended.

### Shaping Deciduous Trees and Shrubs

With deciduous trees and shrubs, you can save much time and trouble in the long run by training them early. Smaller cuts not only require less time, but cause less damage to the plants and reduce the risk of disease. Corrective pruning of mature trees is difficult; it usually takes special equipment and skills to remove large limbs high in the crowns. So, begin training your trees and shrubs at the end of the first

growing season following transplanting. Concentrate on establishing sturdy and healthy branch patterns.

## Pruning at the Right Time

The safest time to prune most trees and shrubs is in late winter, when they are still dormant. Even shrubs that flower early in the year should be pruned then, during or just after flowering. Disease problems are more frequent and severe on shrubs and trees pruned in the fall or during the growing season than on plants pruned in late winter. Another advantage to pruning in late winter is that you can remove any shoots killed by frost. These will have brown, not green, tissue under the bark; scrape the shoot with your fingernail or a knife to check.

Pruning during the growing season has one **advantage:** It is sometimes more effective in slowing new growth, particularly the growth of vertical suckers or water sprouts.

Before you start pruning a plant, study it from several angles to reduce the chances of making a major mistake. Then proceed to remove, in order, dead and damaged shoots, suckers, and crowded shoots. Next, make training cuts. Wait until last to make discretionary cuts for improved appearance. After you've finished functional pruning, you might discover that aesthetic pruning is not necessary.

*Top: There is less risk of disease if deciduous woody ornamentals are pruned in late winter when they are still dormant. At that time frost-killed shoots are also easier to identify and reach. Bottom: Most conifers require little or no pruning, unless you are shaping them. Never shear conifers with hedge trimmers; use a scissor-style hand pruner.*

# Low-Care Flowers

*Because most herbaceous ornamentals don't grow as large as woody plants, they must be planted at high densities. This means that establishing and maintaining flower beds tends to take much more time than caring for woody plants.*

For an easy-care landscape, it's best to keep flower bed areas small. Still, many annual and perennial nonwoody flowers offer reasonably high returns with minimal maintenance. There are some fussy exceptions, of course, but those can be passed over with no regrets—there are dozens of beautiful low-care species and varieties capable of providing a full range of bloom color and timing, size and form, and foliage characteristics.

However, low-care flower beds must be well planned. Poorly planned gardens containing even the lowest-care flowers can require large amounts of maintenance time: Layout is at least as important as plant choice for easy-care flower gardens.

*Smaller, informal flower gardens with fewer varieties and well-defined borders are easier to care for than more formal ones with complicated plantings.*

*An informal, naturalistic garden can be just as attractive as a formal one, and it takes less time and work to maintain.*

## SETTING GOALS

Informal gardens are becoming increasingly popular. By relaxing your standards for a perfect appearance a little, you can substantially reduce maintenance in your flower garden. Trying to preserve symmetrical layouts, with same-sized plants blooming in unison in various parts of the garden, is certain to require much more work than asymmetrical layouts. A slightly lopsided plant won't spoil the visual effect of an asymmetrical garden. Thus, minimal-care flower gardens should be informal, closer to the natural landscape. Leave the formal look to those with professional full-time gardeners!

Even informal flower gardens can become a chore to maintain if they are overly complicated or large. Beginners often make the mistake of trying too many different kinds of flowers in plots that are too large. It's far better to start small, with a few varieties, and then to gradually enlarge the garden by introducing more plants and more varieties.

## PLANNING PERENNIAL FLOWER BEDS

It's important to decide what and where you'll be planting and to have a clear idea of the appearance you want to achieve before you break ground or start to renovate existing beds. Nobody wants to waste time replanning and replanting beds that don't work! The best way to discover planting schemes appropriate to your general area, to your site, and to your own requirements is to observe local flower gardens in yards, parks, and garden centers.

Inquire about those planting schemes that look good to you. What are the species and cultivars? Where can they be obtained? Why were certain plants grouped in particular ways? How much care is needed? Are there ways to reduce maintenance needs? Few gardening books and magazines show low-care gardens. The focus is usually on high-maintenance designs, so don't be tempted to duplicate the exquisite layouts in those publications unless you're prepared to bear the maintenance burdens.

## Start Small

If you're establishing a new flower garden, perhaps to cut down on a high-maintenance lawn area, start small. You'll have plenty of opportunity over the years to enlarge the garden if you discover that you can manage a larger plot. It might be a good idea to establish two or more separate beds in different parts of your garden to take advantage of different conditions, such as shading or slope or soil characteristics.

Establishing a new flower bed is easiest in an area needing little alteration—a flat area with decent soil and no plants requiring removal. However, choosing an easy site doesn't guarantee lowest long-term maintenance. Be alert to light, water, and competition for nutrients from nearby trees and shrubs. Competition can be a particular problem for annual flowers.

Herbaceous flower species, including most of the commonly grown ones, generally perform well in less than ideal conditions, so you don't need to worry about providing excellent soil and precisely timed irrigation. These plants are highly adaptable. Yet, some of the most adaptable species need more care than others. For example, some need periodic replanting, dividing, pruning, thinning, and deadheading (removing spent blossoms). Obviously, you should choose plants that don't need such special attention if you want to spend as little time as possible on maintenance.

## Make Accurate Maps

There are at least two good reasons for making accurate maps of your flower bed plantings before you sow the seeds or start to plant. First, maps will guide you in planting the flowers at the right spacing, helping to prevent gaps and overcrowded spots. Second, if you make careful notes on the maps, they will serve as records for future reference when you're making decisions about maintenance or determining which plants succeeded and which failed. There are simply no substitutes for complete records of your plantings, and the best forms for those records are maps. The time it takes to draw the maps will be repaid many times over when you need to recall which variety was planted where.

### Group Together Plants With Similar Needs

Whether you're planting three or three hundred kinds of flowers, it makes sense to group together those with similar needs to save time on regular maintenance. For example, don't plant hardy perennials next to tender perennials that must be dug up in the fall; removing the latter could harm the root systems of the former. In general, interplanting different species results in more work in the long run than interplanting different varieties of the same species, and yet the diversity of varieties can be just as striking as mixed species.

### Fill In With Annuals

In flower gardens that mostly care for themselves, annuals are best treated as fillers among the perennials. Over the years, as the perennials become larger or multiply, you can reduce the number of annuals. Many of the self-sowing annuals will be crowded out naturally by the sturdier perennials. Consider annuals experimental; if they perform poorly or require too much attention one year, replace them with others the next year.

Annuals are quite inexpensive, whether you start them from seed or purchase transplants, although they do require a lot of planting time in spring, typically about an hour per 100 square feet of bed. If you use self-sowing annuals adapted to your location, you won't need to replant after the first year, but once established, some of these plants are difficult to eradicate.

### Choose Perennials Carefully

Perennials are a different matter. They are more or less permanent and much more costly to replace than annuals. To avoid having to replace perennials, you'll want to plan and choose them very carefully. You should consider the probable size and form of each perennial over a period of several years, visualizing how the appearance of the garden will change over time. If you can sketch views of your plot by using information you've gathered on the

growth rate and ultimate size, shape, and colors of each plant, so much the better.

**Paper-and-pencil trials**   You want to avoid—before it's too late to remedy except with a shovel—entangled shoots, haphazardly intermingling flowers, small plants overgrown or blocked out by large ones, and clashing colors. Strive for balance and proper proportion throughout your plot. Easier said than done, but your chances of getting close to the ideal are much improved by paper-and-pencil trials when in the planning stage, before you start planting.

The basic rules for a visually appealing low-maintenance flower garden are these:
☐ Plant groups of each plant, rather than individuals; odd numbers of plants in each group are more attractive than even numbers.
☐ Place the tallest plants (considering both foliage and flower heights) toward the rear of the bed, and place the shortest toward the front. However, avoid a monotonous stepped profile from tall to short.
☐ Plant along curved, not straight, lines.

*Colorful annuals that are easy to grow from seed, such as zinnias (top) and marigolds (bottom right), make excellent fillers between perennial plantings. For easy maintenance, plan a flower garden so that the taller plants are to the rear (bottom left).*

*Left: Beds of mixed flower colors require less maintenance than beds of matching or contrasting colors. Right: Bricks set flush with the ground make an ideal border.*

☐ For the best effect, place the plants close together. If you must leave extra room around a plant destined to grow very large, fill it with temporary plantings of annuals or even perennials.

☐ Mix flower colors throughout the plot (matching or contrasting color schemes can be breathtaking, but they also almost invariably require much more effort).

If you follow these rules, you probably won't need to rearrange your garden later—at least not drastically.

## Consider Sunlight

Abundant sunlight is important for the best performance of most annual flowers and many perennials. Many species produce very few flowers in full shade. You'll be disappointed if you site a flower bed containing many annuals and sun-loving perennials under large trees or on the north side of the house. A few annual and several perennial flower species will tolerate shade, but they tend to require more maintenance than most of the sun-loving species.

For low maintenance, site beds in full sun and use the lowest-care flower species. If no sunny spots are available or you must choose between putting flowers or vegetables in the one sunny spot, cancel the flower garden (you can always add a few annual flowers to the vegetable garden). If you set up flower beds in the shade, you're asking for extra chores.

## Plan Bed Borders

All that has been said so far in this chapter presumes that flower plants are grouped in beds rather than scattered here and there. Scattered, ungrouped plants in small or individual beds have much greater maintenance needs than do plants grouped in a few large beds. Per unit area, the former have longer borders that require repeated attention, such as edging and debris removal, throughout the growing season. A few large circular beds will have shorter borders than small, irregularly shaped beds with the same total area.

Regardless of how long the borders are, they will need less attention if properly designed. Bricks set flush with the ground or slightly higher are ideal for demarcating the boundary between beds and lawn. A mower can be pushed or driven with two wheels on the bricks, thus eliminating the need for hand-trimming, and the bricks can be hosed or swept quickly to keep the boundary neat. The most maintenance-intensive borders have raised edging, which mandates hand-trimming.

## Provide Access

Another important factor in siting flower beds is access. If you plan to irrigate on a regular basis, be sure that you can make connections to a source of water easily. Moreover, especially during the preparation stages, it will save time if you can bring mulch and soil amendments in bulk directly to the beds in a truck or, at least, in a garden cart or wheelbarrow.

Paving stones can be arranged within a large bed to provide convenient pathways to plants without overly compacting the soil around them. Paving stones can also serve as mulch and are especially well suited to recently established flower beds, where you can use them instead of annuals as fillers between perennial plants. They can be removed readily when you want to add new plants or to allow clumps of perennials to spread.

## Choose Low-Care Plants

Other important considerations when choosing easy-care perennials or annuals include noninvasiveness, cold hardiness, freedom from pests and diseases, and minimal pruning requirements. Easy-care plants do not need staking, and they do not need to be divided or replanted for several years.

## PREPARING THE SITE

Even though low-care herbaceous ornamentals such as those listed in the chart on page 79 will benefit from good site preparation, they don't require it. Only if your site is extremely wet or dry, highly acidic or alkaline, or very low in fertility will you need to take special measures to improve soil conditions. (If you are unfamiliar with the site, you may need a soil test to check the conditions.) Whether you are installing a new flower bed or renovating an old one, improving the soil is less important than getting rid of as many weeds as possible, especially perennial weeds.

*Top left: This strikingly colorful garden probably requires much higher maintenance than a low-care gardener would wish to undertake.*
*Top and bottom right: Large beds with curved borders require less maintenance than many small beds.*

Within a mixed flower bed, there may be some plants more susceptible than others to herbicide injury. After planting don't use post emergence herbicides (which kill plants after they have sprouted), except, perhaps, glyphosate, which you can apply to individual weeds with a hand applicator, a task that can be tedious and time consuming. Be very cautious when applying preemergence herbicides. Preemergence herbicides will kill the seeds of annuals but can be used around transplants.

### Controlling Weeds With Mulch

After the beds are planted, mulching should be your main low-maintenance defense against weeds. Mulch will work well if you make these preparations.

☐ Rid the site of as many weeds as possible during the initial preparation.

☐ Apply appropriate herbicides.

☐ Cover the plot with an opaque material, such as black plastic sheeting, for several months before planting.

☐ Cultivate the plot every few weeks during the growing season prior to planting.

**Traditional mulches**  Traditional particle mulches are most appropriate for flower beds. Chopped leaves, bark pieces, aged sawdust, or wood chips work well. Don't use peat moss, which blows when it is dry, and can form a water-impermeable crust. Don't use fresh sawdust unless you add a nitrogen fertilizer at the same time to keep the soil carbon-to-nitrogen ratio in proper balance.

**Plastic sheeting**  For maximum control of weeds, place perforated plastic sheeting, landscaping fabric, or a similar weed barrier underneath a layer of particle mulch. If you have a drip irrigation system, put the lines and emitters in place before you lay the weed barrier (see the following chapter for details on drip irrigation systems). If you don't have drip irrigation, make sure that the weed barrier lets water through.

Regardless of whether you use a weed barrier, the mulch thickness should not be over 2 inches. If it is more than 2 inches, you risk suffocating the plants. Also, try to keep mulch particles away from plant stems to reduce the risk of rodent damage.

## SOWING SEEDS AND TRANSPLANTING

If you want to grow herbaceous flowers from seeds, use the techniques for producing seedlings described in the chapter on vegetable gardening. Soil blocks are ideal for flower seedlings, especially if they are grown under fluorescent lights or in a greenhouse rather than outdoors.

### Sowing Seeds

When you're sowing seeds directly in beds, you can eliminate the need to transplant all the seedlings by spacing the rows (curved, of course, for best appearance) at the recommended distance for transplants. Then you'll need only to thin within the rows. Sowing and transplanting will go faster if you keep your detailed maps of the beds handy and use a yardstick and string wrapped around pencil-sized stakes to measure and mark plant locations.

### Transplanting

Since your transplants will all be small, a trowel, not a spade, is the best tool to use. Use a knife or scissors to cut holes in weed-barrier material so that it won't interfere with root growth. Except for areas with very small seeds, which can be sprinkled lightly, water transplants and seeded areas thoroughly. Then cover seeded areas with weighted cardboard or pieces of plywood to promote germination (some seeds need light to germinate; don't cover those).

## AFTERCARE

Low-care herbaceous ornamentals generally are so adaptable to soil conditions that you won't need to give a high priority to fertilizing flower beds. Surface-broadcasting slow-release (synthetic or organic) fertilizer is the easiest and safest fertilizing method. If you apply highly soluble synthetic fertilizers, timing and rate are critical for preventing foliage burn.

### Organic Mulch Renewal

Organic mulch needs to be topped off periodically to maintain a 2-inch depth—less frequently if there is a weed barrier under the mulch. When adding mulch, try not to compact the soil around the plants. Paving stones will help to keep all foot traffic in the beds localized to a few spots.

*When transplanting, cut holes large enough in the weed barrier material so that it won't inhibit a plant's root growth.*

# Low-Maintenance Annuals and Perennials

This chart presents species of self-sowing and long-blooming annuals and easy-care perennials that require minimal maintenance.

**Long-Blooming Annuals**
**Easy to Grow From Seed**
Cockscomb (*Celosia cristata*)
Cosmos (*Cosmos bipinnatus, Cosmos sulphureus*)[1]
Gazania (*Gazania rigens*)[1]
Impatiens (*Impatiens wallerana*)[2]
Marigolds (*Tagetes erecta, T. patula*)
Petunia (*Petunia × hybrida*)
Rose periwinkle (*Catharanthus roseus*)[3]
Zinnia (*Zinnia elegans*)

[1] Tolerant of drought
[2] Unusual among annuals, because it grows well in shade
[3] Tender perennial usually grown as an annual
[4] Perennial in warm climates

**Self-Sowing Annuals**
Animated oats (*Avena sterilis*)
Baby-blue-eyes (*Nemophila menziesii*)
California poppy (*Eschscholzia californica*)[4]
Candytufts (*Iberis* species)
Chinese forget-me-not (*Cynoglossum amabile*)
Cloud grass (*Agrostis nebulosa*)
Cornflower (*Centaurea cyanus*)
Flanders poppy (*Papaver commutatum*)
Flowering flax (*Linum grandiflorum*)
Flowering tobacco (*Nicotiana alata*)
Forget-me-not (*Myosotis alpestris*)
Hare's-tail grass (*Lagurus ovatus*)
Love grass (*Eragrostis elegans*)
Love-in-a-mist (*Nigella damascena*)
Meadow foam (*Limnanthes douglasii*)
Pansy (*Viola × Wittrockiana*)
Poppies (*Papaver* species)
Pot marigold (*Calendula officinalis*)
Quakinggrass (*Briza* species)
Red-ribbons (*Clarkia concinna*)
Rocket larkspur (*Consolida ambigua*)
Snapdragons (*Antirrhinum* species)
Squirreltail grass (*Hordeum jubatum*)
Sweet alyssum (*Lobularia maritima*)
Sweet-sultan (*Centaurea moschata*)

**Easy-Care Perennials**
Barren strawberry (*Waldsteinia fragarioides*)
Blackberry lily (*Belamcanda chinensis*)
Coreopsis (*Coreopsis verticillata*)
Daffodils (*Narcissus* species)
Daylilies (*Hemerocallis* species)
English lavender (*Lavandula angustifolia*)
Eulalia (*Miscanthus sinensis*)
Euphorbia (*Euphorbia epithymoides*)
European wild ginger (*Asarum europaeum*)
Fern-leaf yarrow (*Achillea filipendulina*)
Gay-feather (*Liatris scariosa*)
Heliopsis (*Heliopsis helianthoides*)
Hen-and-chickens (*Sempervivum tectorum*)
Japanese anemone (*Anemone × hybrida*)
Magic lily (*Lycoris squamigera*)
Siberian iris (*Iris sibirica*)
Snow-in-summer (*Cerastium tomentosum*)
Stonecrop (*Sedum spectabile*)
Thrift (*Armeria maritima*)
Wild bleeding-heart (*Dicentra eximia*)
Woolly betony (*Stachys byzantina*)

*Use sharp scissors when cutting flowers. In between cuts wipe them with a paper towel moistened with rubbing alcohol to avoid spreading any disease organisms.*

## Watering

Low-care herbaceous ornamentals also are quite adaptable to variations in soil moisture, so you won't have to worry excessively about irrigation timing. Herbaceous ornamentals are low on the list of plants that need routine, heavy watering: Vegetables need most water; trees and shrubs and nongrass ground covers all need more water than herbaceous ornamentals. Only grass can get along with less.

Generally, flowers thrive on 1 to 2 inches of water per week during the growing season, or ½ to 1 gallon of water per square foot per week. If your plants received at least an inch of rainfall within the past week, there's no need to irrigate, unless temperatures and corresponding evaporation rates have been extremely high. Even in a prolonged drought, there's no reason to irrigate at rates higher than 1 gallon per square foot per week, and you can cut down to ½ gallon per square foot per week, or even less, if you need to.

Drip irrigation is the low-maintenance way to water flower beds, but sprinklers (fixed or movable) are acceptable alternatives if water use isn't critical. Sprinklers typically waste about a third of the water through evaporation and runoff. They also wet plant leaves, increasing the chances of disease.

## Staking

Herbaceous perennials that need routine staking have no place in a low-maintenance garden. However, sometimes plants that normally are self-supporting will blow over in storms and you'll have to stake them, at least temporarily. (Later perhaps you'll want to replace them with plants that weren't blown over.) Quick-

staking apparatus is available at garden supply stores, but small bamboo stakes and string might do as well. An easy way to provide support for several flowers in a clump is to surround the clump with several pairs of stakes and crisscross string between them and around the flowers.

## Deadheading

Deadheading, or removing spent flowers, is optional for the low-care plants listed in this chapter. However, the practice isn't very time consuming (you can do it as you admire your flowers), and it makes the plants much more attractive and also encourages them to produce more new buds. Deadheading is of particular benefit to annuals, because they have potential for blooming over a longer period of time than most perennials. Also, deadheading is important for large bulbs, to promote storage of nutrients for use in the following growing season. Deadheading goes quickly if you keep scissors handy when you're walking around the flower garden. Except for camellias and azaleas (because of the possibility of petal blight) don't worry about carrying away the old flowers—just let them fall on the mulch.

## Harvesting

There are even ways to save time when you're harvesting your flowers for beautiful indoor arrangements. Essential are sharp scissors for cutting stems cleanly and one or more small but rather deep water containers for holding the cut flowers and foliage. To avoid spreading disease organisms that you'll have to spend time combating later, wipe the scissors with a paper towel moistened with isopropyl, or rubbing, alcohol between cuts. This precaution is only necessary if you have had previous disease problems or if some of the plants you are harvesting show symptoms of disease.

To reduce the chances of transmitting moistureborne disease organisms from one plant to another, you should wait until the dew is gone to enter your flower garden.

It's a good idea to keep at least minimal records of your harvests so that you can reduce guesswork in subsequent years. In particular, note harvesting dates and outstandingly good bloomers—you might want to plant more of them next year!

## Preparing for Winter

Perennial herbaceous ornamentals that die back at the end of the growing season need to be cut to ground level (annuals can be uprooted). Either break up the debris and spread it over the mulch if there are no signs of disease, or remove it to the trash or a compost pile if it's obviously diseased. A rotary lawn mower chops and spreads small- to medium-sized plants quickly and easily. Even a weed trimmer can handle small plants. In tight quarters you might have to cut and shred some plants by hand. Of course, a power shredder/grinder is ideal for easily chopping up lots of plants in a short time.

You may need to apply extra mulch in the wintertime to protect certain herbaceous ornamentals from hard frosts. Check with your local garden center or extension service for more information about potential frost damage in your area.

## MANAGING PESTS AND DISEASES

Pests and diseases aren't likely to be major problems in flower gardens, except on a few susceptible species. For lowest maintenance remove any particularly susceptible plants as soon as you recognize them. With so many care-free herbaceous ornamentals available, there's no good reason (other than a particular fondness for certain plants) to put up with maintenance-intensive species. Infestations of pests or diseases are highly unlikely if you choose plants from the list of low-care species given in this chapter. Most likely, you'll see some minor damage caused by aphids, scale insects, leaf-eating caterpillars, spider mites, snails, slugs, or a few other pests, but major damage (significantly compromising appearance) will be rare.

### Japanese Beetles

Abundant only in some areas, Japanese beetles can cause severe damage to most herbaceous ornamentals, including those resistant to many other pests. These beetles are efficient defoliators, and heavy infestations need to be treated with appropriate insecticides. Some flower growers have foiled them by covering individual plants or even entire beds with nonwoven row-cover material (available from garden supply stores). Over the long term, local populations of Japanese beetles can be reduced by

applying an organism called milky spore, which kills beetle larvae, to lawn areas. Ask for details on milky spore at your garden supply store if you live in an area where Japanese beetles are prevalent.

### Gastropods

Gastropods (slugs and snails) are quite damaging in some areas, especially in gardens where organic mulching materials are used. Gardeners try many techniques to control gastropods, including baiting traps with beer or milk and surrounding plants with rough materials over which the animals supposedly will not crawl. Two techniques have been found to be most effective: commercially available poisoned baits and copper sheeting placed completely around beds. The sheeting can be quite thin, and should be about 2 inches wide. Apparently, gastropods are mildly shocked when they touch the copper, due to an electrochemical reaction.

### Periodic Checks

You'll save time on pest and disease management if you check your plants periodically. If you spot something that you think might become serious, promptly seek advice from local experts (garden center or extension personnel). It's much easier to spray or handpick a plant or two than fifty plants, so try to catch incipient infestations before they get out of control. Remedial spraying of the entire garden whenever there is the least sign of damage may do great harm to the beneficial organisms in it and aggravate pest infestations. That's why it's often better to obtain expert advice about whether you need to spray.

*Japanese beetles (left) and gastropods (right) can cause severe damage to some plants. Japanese beetles can be controlled with appropriate insecticides, slugs and snails with commercially available baits.*

# Low-Care Vegetable Gardening

*Vegetable gardens run the gamut from sparsely planted, extensively managed traditional layouts to densely planted, intensively managed space-saving designs. These two kinds of gardens require both extra work and care. A low-care vegetable garden fits somewhere between the extremes.*

T he traditional, extensively managed garden covers a relatively large area, much of which isn't directly productive, although it still needs a lot of attention. The space-saving, intensively man aged garden requires extra work and care because the plants have to be precisely spaced and the harvests precisely timed.

*A carefully planned low-care vegetable garden equates food output with the time and work invested in maintaining the garden.*

*Regardless of its size or location, a low-care garden is an efficient one. Compared with a traditional vegetable garden, it produces more food for the time and care invested.*

## SETTING GOALS

A low-care vegetable garden is an efficient one: *Low-care* refers to the time (and, to a certain extent, actual effort) invested for the food produced. A vegetable garden that takes almost no time, but produces practically no food, is not a low-care garden. A vegetable garden that takes a fair amount of time and produces a huge amount of food might justly be called low-care.

No single set of low-care methods is applicable throughout a vegetable garden. Particular methods (some more extensive, others more intensive) for maximizing food output per time invested are appropriate for particular vegetables. Some vegetables aren't even worth considering for low-care gardens, because their food output per time invested is significantly less than that of many other vegetables, even when the most laborsaving methods are used.

In addition to the choice of vegetables, a vegetable garden's maintenance requirements are also greatly affected by how attractive the garden and its produce need to look. Rather untidy vegetable gardens can produce nearly as much food as gardens that look perfect, and the former need much less care, especially less weeding.

Very high standards for produce appearance mandate enormous amounts of garden maintenance time, especially for pest and disease control. This doesn't mean that a low-care garden will look like a weed patch and yield insect-ridden vegetables. Laborsaving methods are available to raise your garden far above a bare minimum level of acceptability, with only a slight addition of time. Your easy-care vegetable garden won't be the most beautiful, and it won't yield the most unblemished produce, but, given the time you spend caring for it, it will provide an enormous amount of food—much more food per time invested than a traditional vegetable garden.

## PLANNING A LOW-CARE VEGETABLE GARDEN

The first step in planning a low-care vegetable garden is to consider how much food you want the garden to produce. This will determine how large the garden should be. Will you be feeding only your immediate family, or do you also plan on providing friends and neighbors with the bounty of your harvests? Regardless of its size and total yield, your low-care garden will demand approximately the same time per unit area. In other words, total time required will be roughly proportional to garden size.

When starting a new vegetable plot, particularly if you're a novice gardener, try to suppress the temptation to break as much ground as possible—remember that more area takes more care! You certainly want to avoid allotting space to vegetables that you won't eat because you've overplanted (12 zucchini plants could feed an army), you've made a poor selection (does anyone in your family *really* like salsify?), or you've planted at the wrong time (it won't do to have the main tomato crop ripen when you're on vacation).

*Lettuce (top left), cabbage (top right), and peppers (bottom) are all high-yield vegetables that have low-maintenance requirements.*

## Using a Map

If your vegetable garden is very small and uncomplicated, you might get by without an accurate map showing the locations of all the plants. Otherwise, a map is essential to guide planting, to identify varieties throughout the growing season, and for reference in later years. A map is especially useful for planning crop rotations that prevent diseases from building up in the soil by not planting the same kind of vegetable in the same area two years in a row. Traditional hand-drawn maps on graph paper are fine, but timesaving computer-generated maps are now possible, thanks to sophisticated garden-planning software designed for personal computers.

## Keeping Accurate Records

One of the advantages of practically all vegetables is that they are annuals, which means that failures aren't disastrously expensive or a long-term maintenance problem. You'll have another chance next year, when you can learn from this year's mistakes. Even so, it's a good idea to keep experiments small in scale and modest in number if you're serious about low-care gardening. Stick with what worked well in the past, and experiment with only a new variety or two to replace poor performers. Accurate records of plant performance are indispensable to making sure you know which varieties worked well and which failed.

*Left: Market and labor forces as well as ripeness dictate when commercial vegetables are harvested.*
*Right: Freshness, taste, and satisfaction are the rewards of harvesting from the home garden.*

There's no need to write down in great detail minor differences in yields; simply record the tremendous winners and the terrible losers so that you don't become confused later about which was which. An easy way to keep records on plant performance is to use 3-inch by 5-inch cards, each devoted to a particular kind of vegetable, arranged in alphabetical order by species and by variety names. You can jot down significant data on the cards, then flip through them later to note good and bad points.

Systematic seed storage can save hours of searching and reorganizing when it's planting time. Consider putting your seeds in alphabetically arranged envelopes and keeping them in an airtight container in the refrigerator (not freezer) for longer storage life. To avoid doubts later, make sure that every seed packet is marked with the year of purchase.

### Timing Harvests

Timing the harvesting of produce intended to be eaten fresh requires a different strategy than that used to time the harvesting of produce intended for preserving (canning, freezing, and drying). For produce that you'll eat fresh, stagger plantings of one variety or plant several varieties that mature in succession. This way you won't be overwhelmed by fresh vegetables that are spoiling before you get to

them. In contrast, you should aim to have the vegetables that you intend to preserve mature simultaneously. Then you can harvest them all at once and preserve them in one batch. Repeatedly setting up the preserving equipment each time you harvest a few vegetables takes effort and wastes too much time.

### Choosing Low-Care and High-Yield Vegetables

A low-care vegetable garden obviously would not include high-maintenance vegetables such as sweet corn, potatoes, eggplant, and pole beans. Growing sweet corn requires preparing and tending a large area per unit food output. Potatoes also require a relatively large area per unit food output, and the rows need extra cultivation. Potatoes are also susceptible to damage from flea beetles and Colorado potato beetles. Eggplants require much coddling because they are very sensitive to low temperatures and extremely susceptible to flea beetle and spider mite damage. Pole beans need trellises, which take much time to construct.

Over the years, several vegetables and herbs have gained reputations for high-food yields with low-maintenance needs. Several of these high-yield plants are listed in the accompanying chart. The species listed are outstanding and require very little care.

*Pumpkin (top left) and corn (bottom left), although popular vegetables, are considered low-yield for the home gardener, because the amount of time and care they need outweighs the amount of food they produce. Tomatoes (top right) and onions (bottom right) are excellent high-yield plants for the home gardener who wants fresh vegetables that require a minimum amount of care.*

## High-Yield Vegetables

These vegetables require relatively little site preparation, have low maintenance needs, but have high food yields.

| | |
|---|---|
| Asparagus | Leaf lettuce |
| Beets | Onions (grown from sets) |
| Bush beans | Peppers |
| Cabbage | Radishes |
| Carrots | Snap peas |
| Chives | Summer squash |
| Dill | Tomatoes |
| Fennel | |

*Plantings in beds or wide rows produce higher food yields than plantings in single rows. The harvest is more bountiful because plant spacings are closer and because uncompacted soil permits better root growth.*

## Designing Rows and Beds

Traditionally, vegetables are planted in single rows with paths between the rows. Single rows are still considered best for some crops, but beds and wide rows are better for others. By using beds and wide rows appropriately, you'll benefit from higher yields, which means you can plant a smaller garden and thus spend less time on maintenance.

The distinction between a bed and a wide row is a little ambiguous: A bed can be considered a very wide row, and a wide row a narrow bed. Beds generally contain more than one kind of vegetable planted side-by-side, whereas wide rows contain only one kind. The important features common to beds and wide rows are block plantings instead of the traditional row plantings, closer-than-traditional plant spacings,

and uncompacted soil in the planted areas. (In the traditional single row, plant root systems are located mainly in the paths, which are compacted by foot traffic and equipment.)

Beds or wide rows can range from 1 foot to 4 feet across, or even more. They should allow comfortable access to the middle from either side to avoid the need to step in the beds, which causes compaction. Three-foot wide rows are well suited to many crops. The chart on page 93 lists several vegetables that are appropriate for growing in wide rows or beds, with recommended spacing between plants after final thinning. Crops sown closer than recommended will cover the soil surface quickly, thus slowing weed growth and soil moisture losses. Then the thinnings of many vegetables can be eaten as early-season treats.

# STARTING SEEDS INDOORS—A VEGETABLE FACTORY

Although you can purchase transplants of many kinds of vegetables, either locally or by mail order, the choice of varieties is limited. To grow some of the best varieties for your location, you'll probably need to start from seed. You'll be trading off the time growing seedlings for time saved later in the season from growing low-care varieties. However, it's doubtful that you'll end up with a net time savings, so buy transplants if saving time is the most important aspect of gardening for you.

If you like growing the best-performing varieties, however, or you enjoy getting an early start on gardening (perhaps planting seed indoors when snow is still on the ground), or you want to control the growth of your transplants, then you should try growing your own.

You can turn a small portion of any room, even the basement, into an efficient vegetable factory capable of producing dozens of transplants in a few square feet. No windows are needed; fluorescent lamps connected to a timer can be set to provide about 15 hours of light per day. The temperature around the vegetable factory can be automatically maintained in the 60s, by adjusting a thermostatically controlled furnace, if you have one, or by placing thermostatically controlled heating mats or wires under the seedlings. Moreover, you don't have to buy containers for your seedlings; all you need is artificial growing mix or potting soil to make soil blocks, as detailed below. You can even arrange for semiautomatic irrigation of the seedlings from capillary mats, as explained later in this section.

## Fluorescent Lamps

The fluorescent lamps for your vegetable factory don't need to be expensive "grow lights"— ordinary soft-white lamps work fine. Devise a way to suspend one or two fixtures containing two 2-foot or 4-foot lamps over a stable flat surface; suspend the lamps in such a way that you can raise them as the seedlings grow—they should always be about 4 inches above the tops of the seedlings. Connect the lamps to an automatic on-off timer (available at hardware stores). Set the timer to turn on at around six in the morning and to turn off at around nine in the evening. This setup will provide around

15 hours of light per day and require very little attention other than occasional height adjustments.

## Heating Systems

If the ambient temperature around your vegetable factory sometimes drops below 60° F (for example, in an unheated basement), you need a heating device. The most efficient way to keep a constant temperature around the seedlings is to place an electric heating mat or wires under the seedlings and a temperature sensor (thermostat) in the growing medium. Also insert a thermometer in the growing medium to measure the temperature; a constant 70° to 75° F is desirable. Heating systems like this can be purchased at some hardware and garden supply stores.

*With an indoor vegetable factory, you can raise transplants of the best-performing varieties during the winter months and get a head start on spring gardening.*

*With a soil-block maker you can create 2-inch-cube soil blocks that are excellent for growing seedlings.*

### Soil Blocks

Homemade 2-inch-cube soil blocks are excellent for growing seedlings. First, you must buy a soil-block maker (available for under $20 from many mail-order seed companies and from some garden supply stores). Next, buy a bag of sterilized growing mix or potting soil. Note that not all growing mixes work equally well for soil blocks. Those with a high peat-moss content work best. You might need to try several different brands and types before finding a really good mix.

To make soil blocks, you simply dampen the growing mix and press it into the four compartments of the soil-block maker, then press the plunger down to push out the finished blocks. They are delicate, so handle them carefully.

### Watering

Top-sprinkling the blocks with a watering can erodes them, and misting by hand requires a lot of time. An automatic misting system works well, but may encourage plant diseases. The best way to water is from underneath, by capillary action.

When you've made your soil blocks, set them side-by-side on a cookie sheet lined with dampened absorbent cloth (such as a towel) that extends a few inches beyond one edge of the sheet.

After you have placed seeds in all of the blocks (don't forget to keep a record of which varieties were planted in which blocks), place the sheet on bricks or similar spacers so that it is elevated a few inches. Then place the dangling cloth into an open-topped container filled with water (glass or metal bread pans are suitable). Water from the container will be absorbed by the cloth and transferred to the soil blocks as they dry out. So all you need to do is to check every two or three days that there is sufficient water in the reservoir.

### Fertilizer

Most artificial growing mixes contain some "starter" fertilizer, but you'll need to add nutrients as your seedlings grow. It's easy to add soluble complete (N-P-K) fertilizer, such as that sold for houseplants, directly to the irrigation water in the reservoirs. Follow label instructions regarding concentration and frequency.

### Modifications

The basic plans for a vegetable factory can be modified to suit your situation and preferences. If you have a greenhouse or even just a large south-facing window, try using natural light instead of fluorescent lamps. You should add supplementary artificial light for a few hours each day if your seedlings are growing slowly and foliage is yellowish because they probably aren't getting quite enough light. If you don't want to make soil blocks, use pressed peat pots or plastic flats as containers. You can devise alternative methods for watering and fertilizing, too.

### Acclimation and Transplanting

Seedlings in soil blocks transplant readily into the garden with little or no shock. To aid the acclimation process, expose the seedlings to

slightly reduced temperatures (around 60° F) for a few days prior to transplanting. Either move the cookie sheets to a cooler spot (still indoors) for a few hours each day or turn down the thermostat setting.

Each soil block has a large volume compared to a standard peat pot or a flat plug, which allows you to grow several plants of some vegetables in a single block. When you transplant the multiple-planted blocks, space them farther apart than if they each contained one plant. Many crops, for example, onions planted 4 to 6 per block, yield well in multiple-planted blocks after being placed in the garden about 6 inches apart. This multiple-planting technique saves time and conserves space in your vegetable factory.

## PREPARING THE SITE

Most vegetables do better in well-aerated, friable soil that has been rotary tilled or hand-spaded. Tilling approximately 6 inches deep is recommended the first time the site is prepared and then, in most cases, again each spring for a few years thereafter. Eventually, due to the cumulative benefits of amending the soil each year, your garden might not require deep tilling or spading each spring. Cultivating or simply loosening the top 2 to 4 inches of soil will be sufficient.

### Tilling in Organic Material

At first, especially if the soil is heavy, don't skimp on deep tilling. It affords an opportunity to mix organic materials thoroughly into the

*Top left: Seedlings also can be started in expanded peat pellets. Bottom left: Seedlings can be classified and grown in plastic flats until ready for transplanting. Right: Rotary tilling to a depth of 6 inches before transplanting aerates the soil, which results in better growth and higher food yields.*

*Sterilization of the soil depends on the heat of the sun trapped under a clear cover. The heat can be intensified by using an insulated row cover.*

upper layers of the soil, which will improve soil aeration and reduce fluctuations in soil moisture. There's no strict limit on how much organic material should be added, as long as the material is well decayed. One inch is a reasonable amount to add to the soil when the site is first prepared and then each following spring. Annually this amounts to about 200 pounds, or 8 cubic feet, of organic material for each 100 square feet of garden area.

After a few years, you probably won't need to mix the newly added organic material into the topsoil; just spread it on top. If you've prepared beds or wide rows, you'll save even more time: You needn't till, cultivate, or spread organic material in the paths, only in the beds or wide rows.

New gardens often replace grass. If that is the case with yours, be sure to get rid of the grass properly, so it won't come back to ruin your vegetable garden. Don't just till it in—that's inviting the grass to resprout from it's roots. Instead, either remove the sod with an undercutting machine (available for rent in many large cities) or use glyphosate herbicide to kill both the tops and the roots of the grass prior to tilling. Herbicide is quicker, easier, and usually cheaper, and it adds beneficial organic matter to the garden soil.

## Controlling Weeds

Weed control should be a major concern when establishing a new vegetable garden. By undertaking a few simple steps in the preparation stages, you can greatly reduce the time you spend controlling weeds later. If you're willing to forego a year's production from the garden, fallow the site for an entire growing season, and cultivate every two to four weeks to destroy the emerging weeds. Alternatively, use both preemergence and postemergence herbicides to kill weeds before you plant vegetables, but be cautious about possible carryover effects. You don't want residual herbicide to kill or stunt some of the crop plants.

## Soil Solarization

A third approach to controlling weeds in a new garden is soil solarization. During the hottest part of the summer, till the soil deeply to make it as loose as possible, then wet it thoroughly. Cover the entire area with clear plastic, sealing it tightly along the edges with soil to prevent ventilation. The heat of the sun will raise the temperature of the soil to sterilizing temperatures in a few days. Leave the plastic in place for six weeks. Solarization not only kills weed seeds, but also cleans the soil of nematodes, diseases, and insects.

## Raised Beds

Deep-digging raised beds each year takes more time than cultivating simple beds or wide rows. Raised beds with plank borders are neat and attractive, but the planks may make a rotary tiller difficult to use unless you set up a special access ramp. Beds raised 2 to 4 inches above the level of surrounding paths have excellent drainage and warm up early in the spring. However, because you don't usually step in raised beds, the soil can remain loose and friable. After working the soil for a couple of seasons, you probably won't need to turn it over, but just rake the surface each spring. Consider raised beds if you like the way they look, if you have heavy, poorly drained soil, and if you plan to irrigate regularly.

## SOWING SEEDS IN THE GROUND

Seeds of most vegetables suited to growing in beds or wide rows can be broadcast by hand quickly without much regard for precise placement. Broadcasting the seed goes much faster than sowing it in single rows with uniform spacings, using a measuring tape or ruler as a guide. Just scatter the seeds as uniformly as you can, stopping when the average distance between seeds is somewhat less than the recommended final spacing. Cover the seeds by pushing soil from the edges of the bed with an upside-down garden rake. You'll never want to return to single-row sowing again!

Unfortunately for growers spoiled by beds or wide rows, several important vegetable crops are better suited to single rows: potatoes, corn, tomatoes, okra, asparagus, broccoli, peanuts, and vine crops such as cucumbers and squash. You'll probably be better off sowing vines (cucurbits) in rows rather than in "hills," because if one of the closely spaced vines in a hill has pest or disease problems, the other vines in that hill are likely to develop the same problems. Regardless of the crop, you won't want to broadcast seed if it's scarce or if you aren't intending to thin the seedlings.

### Single-Row Sowing

When single-row sowing is a must, the greatest time-saver is a push-type mechanical seeder, the kind that sell for about $40 at garden supply and hardware stores. These handle almost any kind of seeds, except very small seeds, which must be pelleted. As you wheel the seeder down the row, it automatically opens a furrow, drops seeds at a preset distance from each other, covers the seeds, and even firms the soil back over them. These lightweight seeders are very easy to use and extremely durable.

Don't be tempted to invest in a larger machine pulled by a riding mower or a small tractor: It will take much more time and trouble, and it can't be used in small areas. Also, don't be tempted to buy a handheld seeder of any kind. You'll waste time because sowing with some types of handheld seeders goes slower than sowing by hand.

### Seed Tapes

Faster than a mechanical seeder are commercial seed tapes, which have seeds spaced along a biodegradable narrow paper strip, ready to be placed in a row and covered with soil. Unfortunately, only a few kinds of seed are available in tapes. If you have time free in the early spring,

## Vegetables Suitable for Growing in Wide Rows

These vegetables are especially appropriate for growing in wide rows. The numbers in parentheses indicate the recommended minimum and maximum spacing between plants. Weed growth will be slowed and moisture losses reduced if plant spacings are closer to the minimum recommendations.

Beans (4″–8″)
Beets (2″–4″)
Cabbage (12″)
Carrots (2″–4″)
Cauliflower (12″)
Celery (8″–10″)
Chard (3″–4″)
Chinese cabbage (8″)
Collards (8″)
Endive (6″–8″)
English and snap peas (2″–3″)
Garlic (3″–4″)
Kale (4″–6″)
Kohlrabi (3″–5″)

Leeks (4″)
Lettuce, head (6″–12″)
Lettuce, leaf (3″–6″)
Mustard (3″)
Onions, from sets (2″–3″)
Parsley (3″–6″)
Parsnips (4″)
Peppers (12″)
Radishes (1″–2″)
Rutabagas (4″–6″)
Southern field peas, including
　black-eyed peas (3″–6″)
Spinach (4″)
Turnips (4″–6″)

you might want to make your own seed tapes by folding toilet paper lengthwise twice (so there are four layers in all), placing the seeds inside at the correct spacing, and then misting the tape with water to seal it. When it's dry, you can roll it up and store it until you are ready to plant it.

*To save time sowing single rows, use commercially available or homemade seed tapes.*

*Composting organic materials at home is inexpensive, but it does require time and labor on the part of the gardener.*

Seeds of carrots and some other vegetables will not germinate through a crusted soil layer. Don't spend a lot of time trying to keep the soil moisture just right for germination. Instead, place plywood or cardboard on the soil to keep it moist, and check every other day to see whether the seedlings are up. Remove the soil covering as soon as the seedlings are visible.

## TRANSPLANTING SEEDLINGS AND TUBERS

When properly hardened-off seedlings are in soil blocks, they transplant without wilting, even in hot weather. You'll probably need to coddle pot-grown seedlings (purchased or homegrown), and you'll certainly need to baby bare-root transplants mail-ordered from another part of the country. All this makes a good case for using soil blocks whenever possible. Most plants suffering from transplanting will start to recover if you provide moderate shade, but don't drape row-cover fabric directly over them—because that can result in too-high temperatures around the plants.

A sturdy trowel is the best tool for transplanting a few seedlings, but a rotary tiller with a furrowing attachment greatly speeds planting a large quantity of transplants or tubers, such as potatoes. The tiller can dig a 20-foot-long furrow in less time than it takes to dig two or three holes by hand. It then takes very little time to set the transplants or potato pieces in place and to hoe soil around them or, in the case of potatoes, over them.

## FERTILIZING

Adequate amounts of organic matter and plant nutrients (nitrogen, phosphorus, potassium, and trace elements) in the soil are important for producing easy-care, high-yielding plants. Supplying nutrients and organic matter can be done in many ways; some are fairly easy, others extremely time consuming.

### Synthetic Soluble Fertilizers

The least expensive and often the least time-consuming way to supply the major nutrients is by using synthetic soluble fertilizers, which are readily available and, being concentrated, easy to handle. The major drawback of soluble fertilizers is that they can damage plants if too much is applied or if the undiluted fertilizer comes into contact with the plants. However, if you follow fertilization recommendations based on soil test results, you should have no problems.

## Low-Solubility Fertilizers

An alternative source of major nutrients is low-solubility fertilizers. These are either synthetic (slow-release coated soluble nutrients) or naturally derived (organic fertilizers, such as bonemeal and blood meal). Low-solubility fertilizers can save you time, since fewer applications are needed during the growing season, but they have some drawbacks. The coated synthetic fertilizers can be expensive, whereas the organic fertilizers are bulky and tend to have low nutrient concentrations.

## Organic Fertilizers

It might be difficult to determine the appropriate application rates for organic fertilizers, because the solubility of the nutrients varies according to soil conditions. Organic fertilizers typically cost significantly more per pound of nutrients than synthetic soluble fertilizers, but less than slow-release synthetic fertilizers. If you're keen to save every possible minute in the garden and cost is no object, use the slow release synthetics. They probably won't save you much more time than soluble synthetics, however.

Recent research has shown that organic nitrogen fertilizers need to be raked or tilled into the soil. This prevents excessive losses of nitrogen to the air as soil microorganisms break down the fertilizer. Since synthetic fertilizers (soluble or slow-release) lose much less nitrogen when left on the soil surface, you can skip the tilling-in step if you use those fertilizers and thus save some time.

## Liquid Fertilizers

Some gardeners apply liquid fertilizer (synthetic or organic) to plant foliage to supplement fertilizer applied to the soil. Diluting and spraying commercially available foliar fertilizer with a small hand-pumped sprayer doesn't take much time. However, because the benefits of each foliar fertilization last only for a short while, the procedure needs to be

repeated several times during the growing season, requiring more time than conventional fertilization.

For your low-care garden, use mainly soil-applied fertilizers that can be applied quite infrequently, such as the slow-release synthetics, which are particularly suitable. Reserve foliar fertilizers for special situations, such as boosting plant nutrient levels during flowering to promote better fruit set or adding trace elements when plants show deficiency symptoms.

## Organic Materials

There are also more and less time-consuming ways to apply organic matter. The most labor-intensive way is to gather plant materials (grass clippings, leaves, and so forth) and compost them yourself. An easier way is to grow "green manure" cover crops in your garden and till them in each spring. Still easier is purchasing organic material and having it delivered to your garden—then all you have to do is spread it over the garden and perhaps till it in.

Even though the last approach is a little more expensive than the other two, it's the clear choice for a garden that as far as possible needs to care for itself. A wide array of organic materials are available in bulk at most garden supply stores: peat, composted manure, topsoil, sanitized sewage sludge, "humus," and sometimes more exotic materials. You're interested in a source of organic matter, not major plant nutrients, so avoid materials with relatively high levels of nutrients.

When you are selecting organic materials, choose materials such as peat (unfortunately,

*Clean, weed-free straw is an excellent organic material to apply to the soil. It makes a good mulch for controlling weeds and keeping the soil moist. A 3- to 4-inch layer provides maximum benefit.*

*Black plastic film used as a sheet mulch provides very good weed control, but it must be cut to fit around each plant.*

one of the more expensive candidates) that break down slowly. In fact, if you apply peat, 2 inches every other spring should be as effective in improving soil tilth as 1 inch each spring of materials that break down faster, such as composted manure and sewage sludge.

Beware of low-cost, bargain organic materials. You don't need materials contaminated by weed seeds or, even worse, heavy metals or other pollutants. If you decide to use sanitized sewage sludge, make sure that it meets government regulations with regard to contaminants. The wrong choice of organic matter may cost time for extra weed control, or, much worse, it may poison you!

## MULCHING

Few herbicides are registered for use around edible crops. Weeds must be controlled by other means. In the vegetable garden, mulch is the key to controlling perennial as well as annual weeds.

You might want to discourage weeds in single-row plantings by tilling with a rotary tiller between the rows a few times during the growing season. Tilling can actually take less time than moving, spreading, and maintaining mulch. However, if you don't have access to a rotary tiller, mulch all of your crop plants—weeding by hand takes much longer. The only exceptions are closely spaced plants in beds or wide rows. These usually provide enough shade to crowd out weeds.

As suggested in the next section, a low-maintenance vegetable garden should have a semipermanent drip irrigation system. The irrigation lines and emitters are most conveniently located under mulch. It's simple to pull the lines out from under the mulch to store them inside during the winter. Moreover, a surface irrigation system needn't interfere with cultivating plants with a rotary tiller. Just keep lines, emitters, and mulch well away from the areas to be cultivated.

## Sheet Mulches

Sheet mulches, such as black plastic film and cardboard, provide better weed control than particle mulches. Particle mulches must be applied very thickly to achieve good weed control, and this isn't recommended because crop plant root systems could be suffocated by poor aeration. However, sheet mulches aren't as easy to apply: They must be cut to fit around existing plants, and cut prior to seeding and transplanting new plants; particle mulches can be moved around easily.

Sheet mulches also aren't very attractive, and they tend to become even less attractive as they deteriorate. The dark surface of some sheet mulches, notably black plastic film, warms the soil and stimulates early growth of certain heat-loving crops. Water-impermeable sheet mulches, such as unperforated black plastic film, require irrigation underneath them, since water applied from above will run off. Nonbiodegradable sheet mulches eventually pose a disposal problem, even if they last for several years. And they don't help improve garden soil, unlike organic particle mulches, which gradually decay. Unfortunately, the least expensive organic mulches, such as straw and spoiled hay, are likely to bring with them at least a few new weed seeds.

## A Combination of Sheet Mulch and Organic Mulch

Using a combination of sheet mulch and organic particle mulch avoids most of the problems resulting from using each separately. A perforated black plastic film covered with a thin layer of organic particle mulch is a nearly ideal mulch for low-care vegetable gardens. At the end of each growing season, the film is

removed and stored indoors until the following spring. Any irrigation apparatus underneath the film is also removed and stored. The particle mulch left on the surface, along with the dead tops of most of the crop plants, is tilled or raked into the soil in the fall.

Since the film is protected from sunlight by the particle mulch, you can choose an inexpensive, thin (2-mil thickness) film. You don't need to be concerned much about ultraviolet stabilization; you can expect two or three years of service from even the cheapest film.

A covering of organic particle mulch makes for a nice-looking garden. It's practical too: It can be spread to cover any gaps in the sheet mulch, it protects the sheet mulch from rapid degradation, and eventually it serves as a source of organic matter for the garden soil.

**The perforated film** Perforated film is available from garden supply stores, or you can make your own by folding unperforated film several times and punching holes spaced on 2- or 3-inch centers through all of the layers with a sharp small nail or large needle. Perforated film allows rainfall to reach plant roots, reducing the need for irrigation. Sheet mulch must be permeable to water unless there are drip emitters under it.

**The particle mulch** The organic particle mulch needs to be about 1 inch thick and can include virtually any particle materials that break down slowly in the soil. Since the particle mulch is separated from the soil by the sheet mulch during the growing season, you don't need to be especially careful about choosing a particle mulch that is free of weed seeds. Some weed seeds in the particle mulch will sprout and die; their roots cannot become established in the soil, since the sheet mulch blocks the way. Other weed seeds will die from exposure to the weather.

Some weed seeds in the particle mulch (probably only a small percentage of the total) will survive, and some of these will sprout in following years. However, in most places, their growth will be blocked by the plastic film. Using both a particle mulch and a sheet mulch also means that you don't have to worry about an organic material with a high carbon-to-nitrogen ratio competing with your crops for soil nitrogen. Even fresh sawdust is suitable,

*Commercial garden centers offer a variety of hoes. Choose one that will work efficiently in your low-care garden.*

since it will have aged considerably by the time it reaches the garden soil in the fall. The following spring you can add extra nitrogen if indications are that it is needed.

**The labor requirements**   The labor needs of this mulching system are simple. After adding approximately an inch of organic material and tilling, raking, or loosening your garden soil in the spring, set the irrigation lines and emitters in position on top of the soil. Roll out the plastic film, punch holes for sowing and transplanting as appropriate, then spread about an inch of organic particle mulch over the film. During the growing season, move the particle mulch as necessary to fill gaps, and hand-weed where needed. At the end of the growing season, rake off and save the 1-inch layer of particle mulch, pull off the film and fold it for storage, remove and store the irrigation lines and emitters, and replace the particle mulch by spreading it evenly over the soil surface.

**Modifications**   There are many possible modifications to the easy-care mulching system. For example, you could place the plastic film in the spring and then wait a few days before adding the particle mulch to allow the black mulch surface time to boost soil temperatures. The particle mulch will provide insulation, keeping soil temperatures high. You could even add an extra layer of plastic film on top of the particle mulch around heat-loving plants.

**A timesaving tip**   Here is a timesaving tip on how to make holes for seeds or seedlings in the plastic film. Never remove sections of the film; always cut flaps that can be folded back (for single small transplants, make two slits to form a cross, so that there are four triangular flaps). Then you can easily repair a mistake with duct tape or simply unfold the flaps wherever a hole isn't needed. This way, you can reuse the film even though your garden layouts change from year to year.

## WEEDING

Even with the best-laid mulch, a few weeds will no doubt slip through. You'll save time by dealing with them while they're still small and fragile. Weeding by hand around the bases of transplants really doesn't take long if your timing is right. Tiny weeds in damp soil take a few gentle tugs, and no more weeds. In broadcast-seeded beds or wide rows, you can rake dense young seedlings to simultaneously thin and weed. This is easy to do when the soil is wet. For single-planted rows, the old reliable hoe and the rotary tiller remain the best and least time-consuming choices.

### Weeding Tools

Various special hoes are available, and you might find one that improves your weeding efficiency considerably, although the traditional design seems to work as well as any. Mini-tillers, available from $100 to $200, are quite effective for cultivation, but not for large-scale soil preparation. Between the hoes and tillers are the push cultivators, which speed cultivation (in fact, they can work faster than rotary tillers) but require a lot of effort.

### Herbicides

Most herbicides aren't appropriate for use around vegetables. DCPA (Dacthal®), a pre-emergence herbicide, is one of the few herbicides labeled for use around food plants. Follow the directions on the label very carefully.

A few post-emergence herbicides, such as glyphosate, can be trusted in the vegetable garden, provided they are applied with precision. Glyphosate, which has low volatility, should be carefully squirted or wiped on individual plants. Make sure you use only herbicides labeled for use around vegetables.

## IRRIGATING

Most vegetables benefit from abundant water, but not from waterlogged soil. The traditional recommendation is 1 inch of water per week, including any rainfall. However, this recommendation has been called into question in recent years by trial results showing improved growth and yields with 2 inches or even 3 inches per week. Unless your soil easily becomes soggy (and even in that case, if your plants don't show ill effects), supplement rainfall with enough irrigation to supply your

vegetable garden with about 2 inches of water each week, possibly less toward the end of the growing season. Two inches amounts to 1 gallon per square foot.

*Power tillers are quite effective for soil cultivation.*

### Drip Irrigation Systems

Installing a drip irrigation system in your vegetable garden can reduce the time you spend on watering to nearly zero. Nondrip semiautomatic irrigation systems, such as fixed or movable sprinklers controlled by timers, can also cut watering time substantially. However, drip irrigation systems have some advantages over sprinkler systems.

With drip irrigation, you'll use less water; typically about a third less than with sprinklers. This is because there is less runoff and practically no evaporation with drip systems. There is also no soil erosion from puddling if you use drip irrigation. Because drip irrigation supplies water at or, in some cases, below the soil surface, plant leaves remain dry, which reduces the chances of disease.

Another significant advantage of drip systems is their competitive pricing, especially if you participate in the design and construction. Do-it-yourself drip systems are also easy to maintain.

**Timers**   A drip irrigation system includes a timer, a valve to prevent backflow of water into your home plumbing, a pressure reducer, a filter, primary lines, secondary lines, and emitters. The details of these devices vary greatly according to the manufacturer, and you need not become too concerned about the differences (except for emitters, as noted below). The end results are similar, regardless of the brand, as long as the emitters don't clog. Although the timer isn't necessary, it saves you many hours a year turning the water on and off.

**Emitters**   The most common complaint about drip irrigation technology, namely that the emitters often become clogged, is gradually being voiced less frequently. The design of emitters has improved, and the new designs rarely become clogged.

Of course, you'll want to use the emitters that clog the least in your easy-care garden, so be sure to question suppliers closely about the performance of the various types of emitters they sell. With sheet mulch over the emitters, clogging caused by debris is unlikely, and an effective filter in the water supply line should eliminate any clogging that is caused by poor-quality water.

**Porous hoses**   The term *drip irrigation* doesn't include punched soaker hoses. Porous hoses made of fabric, white papery plastic, or black rubber have high flow rates compared with drip systems, and the flow rates are hard to regulate and highly sensitive to elevation changes.

Plastic porous hoses are inexpensive but not very durable (expect only two or three seasons of use). They are desirable, however, if you don't have running water at your garden site, since they operate at very low pressure. Rubber porous hoses last a long time but cost significantly more than emitter systems. However, they seldom clog, so are more trouble-free than emitters.

**Flow rates**   Typically, an emitter drips water into the soil at a steady low rate. You can buy emitters that drip at the rate of ½ gallon per hour, 1 gallon per hour, or 2 gallons per hour. The water from an emitter spreads out in the soil; it spreads more in fine-textured soil, less in sandy soil. Lower-flow-rate emitters are more appropriate for clayey soil. Proper emitter spacings depend on plant types and spacings, soil texture, and the flow rates of the emitters. With so many variables involved, it's best to follow the layout instructions provided by the supplier of your drip components.

If your garden receives an inch of rain in a week, you'll want to add an extra ½ gallon per square foot through the drip system. If your emitters drip at the rate of 2 gallons per hour and are spaced 2 feet apart, each emitter provides water to a 4-square-foot area, resulting in a net rate of ½ gallon per square foot per hour. So set the timer for one hour of irrigation. You might not want to provide all of the supplementary water at one time. Emitters tend to clog less if they're used often. Flush the system for a few minutes at least twice a week, even if the recent rainfall has been more than adequate.

**Installation**   Be sure to buy a drip system that has detailed installation instructions. Assembling it should take no more than a couple of hours per 100 square feet of garden area; and you should be able to complete the job with common tools.

You'll install the drip lines and emitters each spring under the sheet and particle mulches. Run lines with emitters evenly spaced along just one side of single-planted rows and wide rows up to 2 feet wide; run them along both sides of wider rows and beds. In many gardens, a uniform spacing of 2 feet between 2-gallon per hour emitters (along the lines and between the lines) won't be far from optimal. Keep the lines out of paths, for safety (and because you don't want to waste water). In the

fall, you don't need to disassemble the system totally, just enough to be able to store it easily inside; the less you take apart, the less you'll have to put back together the following spring.

## MANAGING INSECTS AND MITES

Controlling insect and mite pests, like controlling weeds, takes less time if you start when the infestations are minor. Handpicking a few insects and putting them in a jar of water often is quicker and easier than spraying an infestation later on. Actually, you can start even

before infestations are apparent, by taking preventive measures. There are several approaches to preventing insect and mite infestations, including cultural techniques, mechanical exclusion, and pesticides. Let's consider each of these in turn.

### Cultural Techniques

Cultural techniques can be as simple as growing insect- or mite-resistant varieties of vegetables or as complex as timing plantings to coincide with periods of low pest activity. Other simple techniques include rotating crops

*Porous hoses are more trouble-free than emitter systems because they don't clog as readily. However, the flow rates are harder to regulate.*

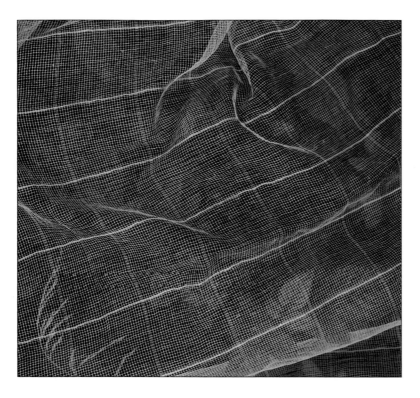

*Mechanical exclusion can take the form of row-cover fabrics or netting. Anchor them at the edges of the planting area after seeding or transplanting. During the growing season allow row-cover fabrics to float on top of the plants so that plant growth won't be restricted.*

to new places in the garden each year and avoiding crops that are most susceptible to pests at your location. Complex techniques include interplanting pest-susceptible varieties with pest-repellent plants and growing "trap plants" to lure pests away from crop plants.

To keep time requirements minimal, you'll want to stick with the simplest techniques: Practice plant rotation in your garden, and grow the most pest-resistant vegetable varieties possible. You can learn about pest-resistant varieties from seed catalogs, extension publications, garden magazines, and from your own experiences.

### Mechanical Exclusion

Mechanical exclusion devices range from the elementary and inexpensive to the highly sophisticated and costly. If you care more about garden production than appearance, "floating" row-cover fabric is the best way to keep major pest insects off plants. Nonwoven white polypropylene is most economical, and it will last two or even three years. It is readily available at many garden supply stores in widths suitable for beds or wide rows.

The labor requirements for using row-cover fabric are not too onerous. You will need to lay the fabric immediately after seeding and transplanting and weight it down at the edges with soil or rocks. During the growing season you

will have to partially remove the fabric occasionally to perform routine maintenance tasks and to harvest the crops. At the end of the growing season, you'll need to remove it for storage or to dispose of it.

If the fabric is positioned loosely over small plants, it will float on top of them as they grow, not restricting them in any way. The fabric doesn't appreciably block sunlight, precipitation, or air flow. A side benefit of row-cover fabric is improved plant growth in the spring, due to slightly higher-than-ambient temperatures under the fabric. Actually, row-cover fabric was originally developed as a means to help extend the growing season (both in the spring and in the fall), not to exclude pests, but for easy-care gardens, excluding pests is the more important application.

In midsummer, floating row-cover fabric can raise temperatures too high for some vegetables. If you notice certain plants wilting under the fabric, raise one side of it during the midday hours to improve the ventilation. This is best done with short stakes attached to the fabric with rubber bands.

Other kinds of row-covering materials can be substituted for nonwoven polypropylene, as long as they let through light, water, and air. However, wire screening and woven fabrics aren't as easy to use and cost more.

## Pesticides and Miticides

Preventive sprays of pesticides and miticides are effective only in terms of killing the few pests (and the pest eggs) you haven't noticed, before the population grows to obvious proportions. In other words, these chemicals don't keep pests away from plants; they simply kill them as they arrive. Although preventive spraying for insect and mite pests sounds like a wonderfully timesaving way to keep vegetables unblemished, it isn't a good idea.

Spraying when pests aren't noticeable can cause more problems later. Sprays can kill beneficial insects that help to keep pests under control naturally. Sometimes pests will develop resistance to the sprays. Spray only when pests are actually present.

**Integrated pest management** Selective spraying is the essence of integrated pest management (IPM), which is gaining wide acceptance among backyard and commercial growers. The full-blown IPM approach involves monitoring pest populations (often with special traps) to decide when to spray. This can take more time than desirable for low-maintenance gardening, but it isn't time consuming to adopt the basic recommendation that sprays should be used only when there is evidence of a developing problem, rather than as preventives in the absence of visible

problems. Save the insecticides and miticides until you really need them.

**Water spraying of mites** There is a dearth of miticides (though many effective pesticides) registered for use on home vegetable gardens. If some of your plants become infested with mites, you'll probably need to resort to some unconventional control tactics. Growers of roses,

*Either a hose-end sprayer (top left) or a compression sprayer (top right) can be used for chemical control of pests. Spraying water (bottom) on plants often gets rid of mites.*

a crop often troubled by spider mites, have found that frequently spraying thin but forceful streams of water on mite-infested leaves (especially the undersides) effectively knocks off many of the fragile mites and reduces the damage caused by the remainder. Spider mites prefer dry habitats.

**Biological controls**   Most biological controls that are available for use in home vegetable gardens require a lot of fuss, including attention to weather conditions and monitoring pest populations for proper timing of the controls. For easy-care gardening, biological controls are best avoided. The one exception: *Bacillus*

*thuringiensis* (Bt), is a bacterium that causes caterpillars of moths and butterflies to stop eating and to eventually die. It isn't toxic to other insects, animals, or humans; there is no waiting period for harvesting crops sprayed with Bt. The single, minor drawback is that Bt needs to be reapplied after rain, because it is easily washed off foliage. To prevent and control caterpillar damage to broccoli, cabbage, and other brassicas, Bt is the low-care choice.

## MANAGING DISEASE
There are two categories of disease management techniques: cultural and chemical. In both categories, the best approaches are preventive

*Opposite and left: Well-planned gardens and proper cultural techniques are the best ways to keep vegetables disease-free. Proper spacing between plants helps to prevent moisture-loving diseases from taking hold; the circulating air dries any wet leaves. Rotating crops each year helps to prevent disease organisms from building up in the soil.*

ones. In fact, for some diseases there are effective chemical preventives but no effective chemical cures once infestations have become established. Thus, unlike pest management, disease management relies largely on prevention.

## Cultural Techniques

Without question, the easiest cultural technique for preventing vegetable diseases is appropriate choice of varieties. There are at least a few disease-resistant varieties of every major kind of vegetable, and new ones are appearing regularly. To attempt an easy-care garden without taking advantage of these would be foolish indeed, so pay attention to the disease-resistance ratings in catalogs and on seed packets when you are choosing vegetable varieties.

**Rotation and spacing**  Rotating crops each year can greatly reduce disease problems, and it takes only a little more time to plan the garden. Various moisture-loving foliage diseases can be prevented or at least minimized by providing ample spacing between individual plants; the enhanced air flow will help to dry leaves wet with dew or rain. Spacing plants too far apart, however, will result in substantially reduced yields per unit area, and it will encourage weeds to grow in the gaps between plants, so don't go overboard. Use exceptionally wide

*Top: Lightweight portable wood and wire frames covered with fabric can be easily placed over rows to protect plants from animal pests. Bottom: Soil solarization effectively destroys disease organisms in the soil.*

spacing only for plants known to be susceptible to foliage diseases.

**Soil solarization** Soil solarization (page 92) is an effective way to destroy many types of soilborne organisms that cause plant diseases.

## Chemical Controls

Out of the vast arsenal of chemicals available to commercial vegetable growers for controlling plant diseases, only a few are registered for home gardens.

# CONTROLLING WILDLIFE

Vegetable gardens are subject to predation by a surprising array of pests other than insects and mites. Such predators range in size—and size of appetite—from the quite small (slugs and snails) to the quite large (deer). Some wildlife predators are more likely to be pests in rural locations—rabbits, woodchucks, opossums, raccoons, and deer. Many are urban dwellers—chipmunks, squirrels, and birds. Their raids on ripe produce can be more exasperating than routine losses to insects, especially when your attempts to prevent such losses are foiled. Many backyard vegetable growers spend more time devising ways to thwart wildlife predation than they spend planting.

The first objective in wildlife control must be to avoid allowing it to become a time sink! This is a difficult objective because most control schemes don't work very well—even "tested and proven" commercial repellents and exclusion devices.

## Exclusion Techniques or Repellents

In general, exclusion works better than repellents. For slugs and snails, a 2-inch-wide band of copper sheeting around the garden is much more effective than crushed eggshells or other sharp materials around the plants. For birds, netting or row-cover fabric placed over plants is much more effective than booming sonic scarers or replicas of owls or snakes. For mammals, fencing is more effective than smelly concoctions or hair hung around the garden.

If your excluders are sturdily constructed, they should require much less attention over the years than repellents, which must be renewed periodically. Invest in durable fencing and netting, and consider placing copper foil at the base of conventional fencing to provide a barrier to gastropods (slugs and snails), as well as to mammals. You will need to invest time to install the excluders and then each year to place and remove the netting, but you'll have few problems with wildlife in the long term.

**Small mammals** The ideal fence for keeping mammals (other than deer) out of a garden is a 4-foot-high woven or welded-wire mesh fence with openings less than 2 inches wide. The bottom 6 to 10 inches should be bent horizontally outward away from the garden and buried 2 or

3 inches below ground, to prevent animals from digging under the fence. The posts should extend far enough above the top of the fencing to allow two horizontal wires with spring-loaded connectors to be attached all the way around the perimeter of the site (even over gates). The lower wire is connected to a standard electric fence charger (available from farm supply stores), and the upper wire is grounded.

Make sure that you buy a charger approved by a safety-testing laboratory, and warn family members and friends to respect the "hot" wire. You needn't keep the charger on all the time during the growing season, but be sure to leave it on at night, whenever no one will be around the garden for a day or more, and all day when produce, especially sweet corn, is ripening.

**Deer**   It's much harder to control deer than other mammals. The prime solution is an 8-foot nonelectric fence or a 5-foot multiwire electric fence. The latter costs less, but either design is quite expensive. Consult your extension agent regarding plans for deer fences. Don't expect homemade or commercial deer repellents to work well for more than a short time. Deer usually learn to ignore repellents very quickly. The best deer repellent appears to be deodorant soap. Soap bars can be hung in cloth sacks tied to stakes placed around the garden at intervals of approximately 10 feet. Its effectiveness, however, depends on weather conditions. The best results can be achieved when the weather is hot and dry.

## HARVESTING

If you follow the recommendations given in this chapter, harvesting is likely to be your most time-consuming gardening activity. That's just fine for most gardeners—harvesting doesn't seem like a chore—but there are ways to save time here, too. Plan your vegetable sowing so that the harvest of each crop is spread over a long time if you're eating the produce fresh or concentrated in a short time if you're preserving. Although it's difficult, try to plant a range of vegetables that won't all need to be picked at once. Even so simple a notion

*Left: The damage to these bean plants was caused by deer.*
*Right: The successful low-care vegetable gardener experiences considerable satisfaction when harvesting healthy high-yield crops.*

as not overplanting can prove a blessing at harvesttime—you'll feel guilty about not harvesting whatever is there, so don't burden yourself by planting vegetables you can't use.

Commercial vegetable-growing operations provide examples of efficient harvesting methods. Their crews are superbly organized, with each of the members assigned a particular task in the harvesting chain. It's unlikely that you'll want to set up a harvest assembly line in your own garden, but you'll benefit by emphasizing systematic, rather than haphazard, techniques.

Don't skip around. Start at one end of a row or bed and work your way down to the other end. Harvest all of the ripe vegetables of one kind before starting to harvest another kind. Have a good supply of containers handy so that you won't have to go looking for more. Most important, use the right tool: A sharp short-bladed knife is the greatest time-saver at harvesttime.

A major part of harvesting is washing the produce. However, with the combination mulching system suggested in this chapter, dirty vegetables are rare. For cleaning root vegetables, an outside sink is a great time-saver, since it won't require much cleaning itself (at least not as much as the kitchen sink) when you're done.

## CLEANING UP

Cleaning up is dull, but unavoidable: The garden needs to be prepared for winter. A proper cleanup includes removing sheet mulch and cutting or mowing off the tops of crop plants. Chopping up plant residues as fine as possible is advantageous, and easy to do with a rotary mower, raised higher than normal if necessary. (But discard diseased plants.) If you have extra time, till or rake particle mulch and plant residues into the top layers of the soil.

Sowing a cover crop (or a green manure crop) to grow over winter will provide an immediate source of extra organic matter that will improve the soil. Cover-cropping takes very little time. Sowing by hand takes only a few minutes, and tilling the following spring should require about the same effort with or without a cover crop. However, it might be necessary to mow off the cover crop before tilling, and if you plan to rake instead of till, it will be more difficult unless the cover crop is first mowed.

A nitrogen-fixing cover crop will reduce the need for nitrogen fertilizer inputs, too. In many regions of the country, a combination of winter rye and hairy vetch (each broadcast at rates of approximately 1 pound per 1,000 square feet) is suitable for providing abundant organic matter and nitrogen. Consult the local extension office for recommendations on the best cover crops.

## Selected Sources for Low-Care Gardening

These sources, though not specifically designed for low-care gardening, can help you with the planning and maintenance of your garden.

**Suppliers of Computer Software Programs for Designing Home Landscapes**
Flower Finder, Infopoint Software, Box 83, Arcola, MO 65603 (417-424-3424)

Gardenview: Mindsun, R.D. 2, Box 710, Andover, NJ 07821 (201-398-9557)

Landscape Plant Manager: Robert Boufford, Biology Department, Ferris State College, Big Rapids, MI 49307

Ortho's Computerized Gardening: Ortho Information Services, Chevron Chemical Company, Box 5047, San Ramon, CA 94583-0947 (415-842-5530)

**Suppliers of Computer Software Programs for Designing Vegetable Gardens**
These programs with detailed maps recommend how many vegetable plants are appropriate for families of various sizes.

CompuGarden: CompuGarden Inc., 1006 Highland Drive, Silver Spring, MD 20910 (301-587-7995)

Gardener's Assistant: Shannon Software, Ltd., Box 6126, Falls Church, VA 22046)

**Mail-Order Companies for Tools and Equipment**
Custom Copper, Box 4939, Ventura, CA 93004 (805-647-1652) (Copper stripping snail barrier)

A. M. Leonard, Inc., 6665 Spiker Road, Box 816, Piqua, OH 45356 (toll free, 1-800-543-8955)

Gardener's Supply, 128 Intervale Road, Burlington, VT 05401 (802-863-1700)

Walt Nicke's Garden Talk, Box 667G, Hudson, NY 12534 (518-828-3415)

Sporty's Preferred Living Catalog, Clermont Airport, Batavia, OH 45103-9747 (toll free, 1-800-543-8633)

## U.S. Measure and Metric Measure Conversion Chart

| | | Formulas for Exact Measures | | | Rounded Measures for Quick Reference | | |
|---|---|---|---|---|---|---|---|
| | Symbol | When you know: | Multiply by: | To find: | | | |
| **Mass** | oz | ounces | 28.35 | grams | 1 oz | | = 30 g |
| (Weight) | lb | pounds | 0.45 | kilograms | 4 oz | | = 115 g |
| | g | grams | 0.035 | ounces | 8 oz | | = 225 g |
| | kg | kilograms | 2.2 | pounds | 16 oz | = 1 lb | = 450 g |
| | | | | | 32 oz | = 2 lb | = 900 g |
| | | | | | 36 oz | = 2¼ lb | = 1000g (1 kg) |
| **Volume** | pt | pints | 0.47 | liters | 1 c | = 8 oz | = 250 ml |
| | qt | quarts | 0.95 | liters | 2 c (1 pt) | = 16 oz | = 500 ml |
| | gal | gallons | 3.785 | liters | 4 c (1 qt) | = 32 oz | = 1 liter |
| | ml | milliliters | 0.034 | fluid ounces | 4 qt (1 gal) | = 128 oz | = 3¾ liter |
| **Length** | in. | inches | 2.54 | centimeters | ⅜ in. | = 1 cm | |
| | ft | feet | 30.48 | centimeters | 1 in. | = 2.5 cm | |
| | yd | yards | 0.9144 | meters | 2 in. | = 5 cm | |
| | mi | miles | 1.609 | kilometers | 2½ in. | = 6.5 cm | |
| | km | kilometers | 0.621 | miles | 12 in. (1 ft) | = 30 cm | |
| | m | meters | 1.094 | yards | 1 yd | = 90 cm | |
| | cm | centimeters | 0.39 | inches | 100 ft | = 30 m | |
| | | | | | 1 mi | = 1.6 km | |
| **Temperature** | °F | Fahrenheit | ⁵⁄₉ (after subtracting 32) | Celsius | 32°F | = 0°C | |
| | °C | Celsius | ⁹⁄₅ (then add 32) | Fahrenheit | 212°F | = 100°C | |
| **Area** | in.² | square inches | 6.452 | square centimeters | 1 in.² | = 6.5 cm² | |
| | ft² | square feet | 929.0 | square centimeters | 1 ft² | = 930 cm² | |
| | yd² | square yards | 8361.0 | square centimeters | 1 yd² | = 8360 cm² | |
| | a. | acres | 0.4047 | hectares | 1 a. | = 4050 m² | |